STRENGTHENING K–12 SCHOOL COUNSELING PROGRAMS

A Support System Approach
Second Edition

Donald R. Rye, Ed.D.
Rozanne Sparks, Ed.D.

USA	Publishing Office:	ACCELERATED DEVELOPMENT *A member of the Taylor & Francis Group* 325 Chestnut Street, Suite 800 Philadelphia, PA 19106 Tel: (215) 625-8900 Fax: (215) 625-2940
	Distribution Center:	ACCELERATED DEVELOPMENT *A member of the Taylor & Francis Group* 47 Runway Road, Suite G Levittown, PA 19057-4700 Tel: (215) 269-0400 Fax: (215) 269-0363
UK		ACCELERATED DEVELOPMENT *A member of the Taylor & Francis Group* 1 Gunpowder Square London EC4A 3DE Tel: 171 583 0490 Fax; 171 583 0581

STRENGTHENING K-12 SCHOOL COUNSELING PROGRAMS: A Support System Approach, Second Edition

1 2 3 4 5 6 7 8 9 0

Printed by Edwards Brothers, Ann Arbor, MI, 1998.

A CIP catalog record for this book is available from the British Library.
∞ The paper in this publication meets the requirements of the ANSI Standard Z39.48-1984 (Permanence of Paper)

Library of Congress Cataloging-in-Publication Data

Rye, Donald R., 1940-
    Strengthing K-12 School Counseling Programs: A Support System Approach / Donald R. Rye, Rozanne Sparks. -- 2nd ed.
        p. cm.
    Includes bibliographical references (p.   ) and index.
    ISBN 1-56032-689-1 (case: alk. paper)
    1. Educational counseling -- United States. 2. Counseling -- United States. I. Sparks, Rozanne, 1946-   . II. Title.
LB1027.5.R94 1998
371.4--dc21   98-29620
                                                          CIP

ISBN: 1-56032-689-1 (paper)

STRENGTHENING K–12 SCHOOL COUNSELING PROGRAMS

TABLE OF CONTENTS

LIST OF FIGURES

FOREWORD

Practical. Commonsense. Usable. Accountable. Job-saving.
These are some of the words that come to mind to describe the
second edition of Donald Rye and Rozanne Sparks's *Strengthening K–12 School Counseling Programs: A Support Systems Approach.*

Having had the opportunity to share the first edition of this
book with my professional school counseling interns and their site
supervisors at Mankato State University, I can personally attest to
the accolades both groups awarded the concepts advanced by Don
and Rozanne in this comprehensive stakeholders approach to guidance and counseling program development and management.

Society demands that professional school counseling—whether
viewed as a component of the overall curricular mission of the
school or as an add-on support program—must be able to validate
what it does, for whom, and how well it achieves its stated goals.
Those who apply the Rye and Sparks model will be able to answer
all three of these critical questions and may, in the process, provide the evidence that school counseling services are worth continued funding in this era of decreased funding for K–12 education.

There is a story I tell to my students about a new school district superintendent who decided arbitrarily to eliminate the school

counseling program. The attempt proved a dismal failure. Because the school counselors had an advisory board of parents and other interested community members who advocated counseling services, because they had evidence of the effectiveness of their services, and because they were valued and esteemed members of the overall curricular mission of the school district, the superintendent was forced to retract the original decision. In fact, after the dust had settled, the district ended up *adding* school counselors.

In another school district, however, the story turned out quite differently. The same decision was made to cut school counseling and guidance programs. But the counselors there had no advisory board, no evidence of the effectiveness of their program, and no true sense of integration of services among the teaching and administrative staff. Consequently, that school district offers no counseling services today.

In this book, you will find other real-life examples and information on relevant materials and approaches for delivering effective counseling services within a school curriculum. The sample evaluative instruments for the elementary, middle, and secondary school levels remain the book's main attraction for both interns and practitioners. And the authors' emphasis on the need for strong advisory committees to assist and advocate for comprehensive K–12 guidance and counseling services continues to ring loudly throughout the text.

School counselors in training and practitioners alike will benefit greatly from the ideas and examples in this edition. And the most important shareholders in the world of K–12 education—students and their parents—will benefit from the improved counseling and guidance services that will emerge through the implementation of the Rye and Sparks model.

And isn't that what we are all about?

Walter B. Roberts, Jr., Ed.D., L.P.C.
Associate Professor of Counselor Education
Professional School Counseling Program
Mankato State University

ACKNOWLEDGMENTS

We want to thank all of the counselors who have invested time and energy in planning and managing counseling programs like the ones in this book. Thanks to Kay Melton and Dr. Ellis Melton for their efforts in implementing the process in an international setting. A special thanks to Laurie Carlson, Ph.D. candidate at the University of Arkansas, for reading the text and making recommendations and for her editorial assistance.

It is a real honor to have Rebecca Groves Brannock, Ph.D., write a chapter for this second edition. Becky was Rozanne's student at Pittsburg State University, and Don's student at the University of Arkansas. She is a rising star we are proud to have as a colleague.

We greatly appreciate the support we have received from Walter B. Roberts, Jr., Ed.D. His sharing of ideas and suggestions for uses of the book in graduate school counseling courses have been invaluable.

Chapter 1

STRENGTHENING K–12 COUNSELING PROGRAMS

The aim of this book is to help practicing school counselors, counselors in training, school administrators, and other members of school communities to develop or strengthen comprehensive developmental school counseling programs. We hope the content will serve as a guide for institutionalizing a process for planning, implementation, and evaluation that will last for years. This information can help in designing an individualized planning and development process within a school district (K–12), at a specific grade level (elementary, middle, secondary, or postsecondary school), or at an individual school.

BUILDING STRONG FOUNDATIONS

Strong systems, whether physical structures or human institutional endeavors, begin with solid foundations. A school system is no more stable than its base of community support. For the most part, that community support is earned. However, support may become increasingly fragile if student, parent, and community expectations are not met. So to build strong community support,

1

educators must install a continuous feedback and involvement loop for each key component of the school. Finding ways to solicit, value, and incorporate the opinions and expertise of community members is the key. When such support is solicited, valued, incorporated into decisions, and makes a noticeable difference, it becomes a reliable and solid foundation upon which to build. The most fundamental base of support for any institution is derived from the values and ethical commitments held by members of the surrounding community and demonstrated by members of the institution itself.

A strong school counseling program requires an intentionally framed system that brings together the community, the school, and the counselors. Folks within a community support each other and work together when they know that their values and beliefs are understood and supported. When the community reaches a consensus on the core values underpinning school efforts, members can more easily agree on what is to be done, how it is to be done, and what should result from the actions taken. With a solid foundation of values and a coherent system of school and community support, the school counseling program will grow stronger.

Disciplined, consistent pursuit of an effective and efficient school counseling program built on agreed-upon values makes possible a shared vision and a focused mission. Transforming the school counseling program from a hodgepodge of activities to a continuously improving system of strategies with predictable effects is the goal. School counseling programs are strongest when the most fundamental human needs are understood, and when honest efforts and clear plans are made to meet them. The counselor's efforts to meet those needs are best supported by a community-based team effort.

SCHOOL–COMMUNITY TEAMS

When school-community teams work together to design comprehensive programs to meet identified needs, the results are coherent efforts rather than fragmented and competing ones. Career, drug and alcohol, sex, and parent education; crisis intervention;

suicide prevention; and services to at-risk students are most effective when they are integral parts of a comprehensive K–12 counseling program. But the needs targeted by special programs often are determined by funding sources and the bias of persons outside the local community. School counseling programs that are solidly based on evidence of need can incorporate these special programs into a planned program so that the efforts of counselors, teachers, and administrators are extended rather than diverted. A fully functioning system of counseling and support services requires all members of the educational community, as well as selected individuals and groups from the larger surrounding community, to work together to support each other.

BASIC BELIEFS

What we have come to see clearly is that debate and discussion will not resolve questions about the role and function of the school counselor. On the contrary, continuing that debate only gets in the way of the proactive designs that can bring strength, coherence, and excellence to school counseling. We hope the information in this book will help school counselors and others to build strong developmental and comprehensive school counseling programs.

This book is based on some fundamental beliefs:

1. Governing values are the foundation of all human endeavors.

2. Education is the top priority for ensuring a positive future for all of us.

3. Comprehensive counseling programs are essential elements of any quality educational process for students.

4. Quality counseling programs must be developed from explicitly stated value bases and have both administrative and community support.

5. Comprehensive services must be systematically planned, implemented, and evaluated over an extended period of time.

6. Program planning is most effective when it is centered in an informed team of school and community representatives.

7. Effective counseling programs are specifically designed to meet identified needs in the school and community populations.

8. Programs of excellence offer services that build self-understanding and a variety of skills in a pattern of increasing levels of difficulty as students move from grade to grade.

We hope this brief guide will encourage you to engage in a process that will lead to the transformation of your school counseling program. Admittedly, only the most dedicated, committed, and insightful professionals will invest the time and energy required to accomplish the ideals set forth here. Those who choose to initiate this change strategy will be richly rewarded by their own sense of accomplishment and the success of others caught up in the work of directing the future of our profession. Above all, the most fundamental values we hold in this profession will be perpetuated, students will benefit, and we will have participated in creating a better future for humankind.

WHO CAN USE THIS BOOK?

This book can be used as a preservice text to help counselors-in-training learn a team-centered collaborative planning process and the technical aspects of needs assessment, goal setting, implementation, and evaluation. Graduate students may be divided into simulated advisory teams and directed through the planning process as they learn the skills and complete a sample five- or six-year plan.

Used as a guide to planning, this edition can help extend and refocus the efforts of school staff. The process described here and some of the activities can improve any component of a school program.

The detailed and specific ideas in this book also can be used by a single counselor in one school. This edition gives special attention to defining beliefs and values as a basis for planning and underscores the importance of a shared vision and defined mission.

The current movement in most states toward comprehensive developmental school counseling program planning and management has resulted in various state mandates and guidelines. While the emphasis varies from state to state, most professionals agree that community-based decision making is essential. This guide can help you structure the planning process within the framework of any state. It provides a format by which a community-based planning process can be institutionalized.

Chapter 2

WHY PLAN?

Developing quality school counseling programs has been a goal since the beginning of school counseling. The early years of growth in counseling was characterized by questions such as "should the counselor serve as a screening and recruiting agent for the nation?" and "how should this function be carried out?" More recently, the primary questions have been "should the counselor be an individual therapist or provide classroom preventive and developmental guidance?" and "should the counselor focus on career education, drug education, sex education, and at-risk youth?"

COUNSELING PROGRAMS CHANGE OVER TIME

School counseling programs have been evolving for decades. We have seen marked changes in emphases alongside shifting social, economic, and political agendas. Social experimentation and challenges to the institutions of religion, government, and education in the 1960s brought an emphasis sometimes called the *human potential movement*. The personal freedom expressed during that period sparked political and economic alarm that the work ethic of the United States was threatened, resulting in the *career education movement* of the 1970s. By the 1980s, concern over teen pregnancy, drug and alcohol abuse, violence, and global economic competition led to competing emphases for school counselors. The *school-to-work transition* emphasis has made economic competitiveness and worker productivity a high priority, while teen pregnancy, family violence, and drug use convinced many that a *mental health movement* was needed in school counseling.

Counselor educators, state department of education supervisors, and practicing school counselors have written articles, held discussions, and done research trying to explain what the counselor is to do within the school. For example, participants at a 1987 conference called *Building Strong School Counseling Programs* reviewed 20 years of history and proposed issues for the next 20 years. Discussions from that conference illustrate the value differences and motivations for change within our ranks.

Capuzzi (1988), for example, emphasized helping students develop personal and social skills for the future, while Griggs (1988) emphasized facilitating learning and understanding the politics of education. Gysbers (1988), on the other hand, claimed "the nature of our professional commitment rests squarely on what career development and career guidance means today" (p. 108).

The lack of clarity about our profession was shown by Loesch (1988), who said counselors are unsure whether "the school counseling profession's efforts have been, are, or will be successful" (p. 169), and by Cole (1988), who suggested, "the whole issue of just what is the school counselor's responsibility needs more debate" (p. 143).

These varied opinions on the focus of the future suggest some divergent governing values—individual development (Capuzzi), learning in an educational context (Griggs), and career development and guidance (Gysbers)—while Loesch and Cole suggested it is not yet clear. Creating a vision of the future from these disparate governing values might result in at least three distinct pictures. For example, the vision represented by Capuzzi could be called the "psychological consultant"; that of Griggs, perhaps, the "curriculum consultant"; and Gysbers's, obviously, is "preparation for work." We suggest that all are relevant to the work of the school counselor; we must search for the value set that encompasses all of these positions so we can create a clear vision of where we want to go while remaining connected to the strengths of our past.

The search for the optimum "future" of the school counselor has continued for more than 50 years. Consequently, many individual counselors, school administrators, and teachers have adopted one or more of the various views. The results have been programs based on the strengths and interests of individual counselors, the biases of counselor educators, state department of education requirements, or the administrative needs of the local district.

Less-than-prepared persons have sometimes filled counseling positions and managed to put together programs based on collections of ideas and materials from a hodgepodge of sources. Such incoherent efforts have confused students, parents, teachers, administrators, and even counselors themselves. These programs have held out a promise of help for students but sometimes failed to produce positive outcomes.

The responsibility for developing and implementing school counseling programs rests with school administrators, and they may not completely understand or know how to support counseling in their schools. Persons who have yet to complete counselor preparation programs often are assigned quasi-administrative tasks. But simply leaving the school counseling program in the hands of a professional counselor may build in a bias toward mental health work, career guidance, academic excellence, obtaining college scholarships, class scheduling, or some other set of activities because the counselor happens to hold a particular bent or expertise and favor such in her or his work. To build a strong and balanced program, the administrator and counselor must work together.

COUNSELING PROGRAMS DIFFER FROM COMMUNITY TO COMMUNITY

Those who assume that professionals can best determine priorities overlook a fundamental premise of the counseling profession: that counselors must begin with their clients' understandings of their own situation. Even within the medical model, physicians never attempt a diagnosis without gathering extensive information from the patient. Obviously, this process increases the likelihood that the treatments chosen will be appropriate. Most counselors are committed to this belief and are aware that the only way to bring about change through the counseling process is to "start where the client is," *not where the counselor is.*

It follows that programmatic efforts are most likely to be effective when they are responsive to the population served. If we are to focus our efforts on the strategies most likely to result in positive outcomes for our clients, we must learn what it is they seek. Simply allowing administrators to determine how we will function, or allowing individual counselors to play out their own biases or to simply wait for what comes through the door, abdicates our responsibility as professionals. We will only achieve the influence we seek, the recognition we deserve, and the quality our clients demand when we go beyond these approaches to planning.

COUNSELING PROGRAMS DIFFER
ACCORDING TO NEEDS

We propose an approach that rests on the assumption that *clients are in the best position to determine the nature of their own needs.* Recognizing that a program is designed to serve needs means the program will change as the needs do. Starting with this assumption acknowledges that counselors are trained to offer a set of specialized services aimed at facilitating human development and remediating developmental problems. It also argues with the notion that professional training is sufficient preparation for interpreting client needs without significant inquiry into the particular characteristics of each client or community system.

Therefore, planning must include a consumer-based effort to identify, in a systematic and locally meaningful way, the particular counseling needs within each school district. A consumer-centered program requires a community-based planning and development effort. Community-based decision making ensures involvement with and commitment to locally identified issues of concern.

Once a study of expressed needs has been completed, and the results analyzed and understood, the debate over the school counselor's role is no longer relevant. *By definition, the counselor functions to meet the identified needs that fall within his or her areas of expertise.* It remains an administrative decision whether any individual counselor has the necessary qualifications to deliver those services. Furthermore, the administrative decision about which combination of competencies from which individual counselors will best match the approved plan then becomes clear, and hiring or retraining of existing personnel proceeds with purpose and focus.

Comprehensive developmental counseling programs will evolve toward an increasingly sharpened focus when they are coherently attuned to the interests and needs of the consumers they serve. This process of continuous improvement can best be initiated and sustained by an informed body of community members engaged in program planning, implementation, and evaluation: in other words, *an advisory team.* This advisory team provides a link with various consumer groups and the personnel and activities of the counseling program. It also provides for parent representation from all grade levels, as well as from teachers, administrators, the school board, and the community.

ADDRESSING NEEDS FROM A COMPREHENSIVE-DEVELOPMENTAL MODEL

To provide continuity throughout the counseling program, you need a district-wide (K–12) planning and development effort. A comprehensive developmental program of services rests on the belief that human development is sequential and that developmental tasks mastered at an earlier stage of development are necessary for mastery of subsequent tasks.

An example of this sequencing can be seen in the concept of life career development, which emphasizes learning through stages: career awareness (self-awareness skills) in grades K through 6; career exploration (career awareness skills) in grades 7 through 9;

and career preparation (job or college preparation skills) in grades 10 through 12. Clearly, the decision-making skills required in high school are built on the skills mastered in elementary and middle school.

If a career education program does not build on early competencies and previously developed skills, then later programmatic efforts will not be effective. It is as important to plan coherent, sequential counseling programs as it is to plan the sequential development of math or grammar skills.

AN INVESTMENT OF TIME AND EFFORT

All consumers benefit from a well-planned comprehensive developmental program. However, the time (five to six years) and energy required for planning, implementing, and evaluating such a program are extensive. Such a program requires an investment and commitment by many people and strong leadership from the counseling professionals in the school. But the benefits are immense.

Students benefit because the program offers a full range of counseling services—personal, social, educational, and career.

Parents benefit from being involved in educational and career decision making with their children, and from access to counseling services.

Teachers benefit from having a team partner who can provide specialized assistance in improving student learning and personal adjustment.

School board members benefit because they are able to communicate aims, purposes, and operations of the counseling program to the community.

Business, labor, and *industry* benefit from having an avenue for collaboration with the school that can result in more positive career education efforts.

Administrators benefit because they are able to provide a stronger position of support through management and evaluation when the planned counseling program has community and school board backing.

The school board's approval of a comprehensive plan will help ensure year-to-year continuity. Continuity in services delivered to all students is essential in order to build skills sequentially. Many counselors have experienced the unfortunate effects of administrative changes on the work they do. One counselor we know considered engaging her school and community in a comprehensive planning effort, but decided not to because of the tremendously positive support she had from a competent and progressive building principal who encouraged and supported her efforts. Soon, however, his competence and expertise were rewarded—and he became the superintendent in another school district. His replacement had little understanding of school counseling and directed all of the counselor's time toward administrative tasks, including the sale of school supplies in the central office during lunch. The counselor's attempts to gather support from others were unsuccessful, and soon she became so discouraged she left education, moved to a large city, and began working for a major corporation. A very different result might have been possible if the school board had approved a master plan. With school board approval, the counselor would have had administrative support to help persuade the principal.

SUMMARY

Professional counselors benefit from an overall, comprehensive, school board-approved program. Having a clear mission with structured goals allows counselors to make full use of their knowledge and skills, fosters higher morale, reduces stress, and promotes quality efforts as counselors become effective members of the educational team. Planning establishes direction and focus, leads to recognition and support, makes possible meaningful evaluation, and permits all stakeholders to participate in the process.

Chapter 3

FOUNDATIONS FOR PLANNING

As members of the educational community, we are charged with transmitting knowledge and culture; developing learning skills, work attitudes, and work skills; and perpetuating our society's core values.

In the past several years, we have heard increasingly urgent cries of dissatisfaction at the way we are fulfilling our obligations to our students in this country. Calls for systemic reform in American schools have come from many quarters. Some believe our public schools have failed to teach the competencies and qualities needed for a world of increasingly interdependent economic, political, cultural, environmental, and social relationships—that we must change ourselves in fundamental ways in order to sustain ourselves and create a positive future.

Research, local planning, teacher preparation, restructuring, new models of leadership, corporate management of schools, and curriculum reform are some of the efforts underway to discover the best means of preparing our youth for the next century. A central question we must address is this: How do we encourage enough learning, enough understanding, and enough awareness so that our youth are equipped to find solutions to problems and seek new directions for the interdependent global future of humankind?

The core responsibility of our school counseling profession is to help individuals, groups, families, and schools as they seek more effective ways of managing their education, personal development, and interpersonal relationships. We know that the heart of our work is helping our clients select and create a future for themselves as well as manage the effects of the present and the past. We also know that our clients are sometimes adrift in the complexities of their lives as they learn to think, feel, behave, and want appropriately.

A rapidly increasing pace of change in the world of work, global interdependency, technology, communication systems, education, the social agenda, and political landscapes requires that families, individuals, and groups plan more effectively, focus more clearly, and produce more efficiently. These demands increase the stresses felt by almost everyone. Increasingly, professional counselors are called to provide the assistance needed to reach the optimum levels of functioning across a lifelong process of learning.

COUNSELORS' PROFESSIONAL IDENTITY

The help school counselors provide becomes increasingly important as the complexity of the problems and decisions faced by students and their families increases. Moreover, counselors often feel caught between the demands of competing interest groups who hold opposing values on child rearing, education, alternative lifestyles, and appropriate personal behavior. Certain developmental understandings and specific counseling techniques are opposed by some lay and professional groups. Opposition and argument are particularly troublesome when voiced by influential persons in a community who don't understand developmental stages, don't see the contribution counselors make, and don't have the expertise to provide counseling services in the school.

In spite of the many difficulties, counselors continue to seek effective and acceptable methods to deliver the services needed by students, parents, teachers, and administrators. Clearly, the demands on school counselors have increased as we are asked to provide assistance for increasingly difficult human problems rising out of the changes we all are experiencing. *Many school counselors feel they can no longer afford the luxury of listening to students,* even though listening may be the most powerful means of ensuring normal growth and development. Some elementary school counselors spend 90% of each week teaching preventive lessons in classrooms, and some high school counselors devote most of each day to getting students into college on scholarship. Other counselors give up or resort to one or the other of these activities as a way of coping; they simply cannot be all things to all people.

Delivering a comprehensive developmental program of services means finding time for individual and small group counseling with students; consulting with students, parents, and teachers; and maintaining referral sources, classroom preventive guidance, college planning, and a myriad of other tasks. In short, the demands are many and complex and the level of quality and expertise now required to do this work is higher than ever before. With more needs than can be met and too little time to respond to all demands, it is imperative that the very best planning occur so that we can make maximum use of all available helping resources.

But how can we plan to do "first things first" when everything seems to be a first thing? How are we to provide the services most consistent with the values of our profession, particularly if they are in conflict with those found in our communities? How do we prepare our students for a future yet unknown? More importantly, how do we equip them for creating a survivable future for humankind? While such questions are abstract, they are fundamental.

FINDING A FOCUS

Bringing our planning efforts into concert across a broad base of community and school representatives will improve our chances of grappling successfully and systematically with the fundamental questions of our future. The first step is to examine the particular contextual issues of the school community. Many of these issues are assumed or obvious; they may have been included in previous planning and decision making throughout the school.

However, the profession of school counseling is still relatively new and diverse; bringing into focus the essential elements appropriate for each school community requires extensive and deliberate attention. Finding a clear focus comes from making many adjustments and accommodations throughout the planning process and is closely related to the early steps of the process. Having a solid base of articulated values, a clear and shared vision, a well-defined mission, identified priority needs, and achievable goals gives us a framework to build on as we help our students create their futures.

FINDING THE BASE

Perhaps it is pointing out the obvious to suggest that our way of life in these United States has rested on a set of democratic ideals and governing core values first articulated in the Constitution. In all cultures of the world, core values rest at the root of each political and social system. Values and ideals in the United States provide the basis for the "American Dream." They are the markers by which individuals dream and groups envision the future.

Core Values

Core values—whether or not they are explicitly stated and consciously understood—motivate and guide human activities within each socially and culturally bounded system. Social, political, and institutional boundaries are established when a common set of core values exists within the system and support is given for those core values within surrounding systems. Groups with similar cultural roots evolve policies, decisions, and activities to reflect their own core values and thereby form a bounded system capable of producing a vision of the future. Core values are symbolized and institutionalized in politics, education, economic activity, religion, the arts, and in relation to other bounded systems. The values and ideals of every culture, social system, and institution around the world have been articulated and institutionalized through the endeavors of the people within their identifiable boundaries. Governing values provide the foundation from which policies, decisions, and plans bring focus to a vision of the future.

Inevitably, however, you will find within each system various interpretations of how core values are to be prioritized, articulated, and transmitted. When disagreements about appropriate interpretation are strong, and the mechanisms for negotiating the differences are present, explicit, and agreed upon, the system is functional. However, when groups with divergent core values press for adoption of their particular interpretations, and the mechanisms for negotiating differences are absent, conflict is likely.

The presence of serious value differences and the absence of an effective means of resolving those differences will result in conflict over the elements, means, and priorities given to transmitting the culture. Power struggles and their attendant disruptions may interfere with the most fundamental system functions, and the system may be unable to sustain itself. Stated differently, when internal conflicts disrupt a system's most essential institutions (government, economic, and social), the resulting chaos leads to significant dysfunction and the system can no longer sustain order, transmit a coherent culture, or create a future. Systems that are unable to function for extended periods of time are placed at risk for extinction. The crisis created by possible extinction may lead to a series of corrective adjustments based on new institutions for sustaining values or to a transformation of the system based on some new paradigm of core values. Generally, however, dysfunction becomes critical when the core values are in dispute and resolution of the conflict is not forthcoming.

Conflicts between bounded systems arise when their governing values clash. Unless bounded systems find a meta-position of core values that are more universal and acceptable, conflict continues.

Incidentally, one source of increased stress in the global arena is the fact that, even while boundaries are becoming less well-defined, they are more easily penetrated by new communication technologies. Individuals and groups now readily communicate across once impervious boundaries created by governments and other institutions that sustained the integrity of the cultural system. With less clarity in the boundaries comes more uncertainty that the system will maintain an identity sufficient to meet the security needs of its members. The most obvious symptom of such disruptions may be seen in the increased efforts of violent terrorists. Terrorism turned toward the established institutions within a system indicates that anxiety among some individuals is high, and that a return to the safety of a simple and clear set of defined values is desired by those most threatened.

A similar disruption occurs within organizations. For example, failure to hold a shared and coherent set of values, coupled with a lack of mechanisms for resolving values differences, often leads to subgroupings within an organization. If the basic values are not renegotiated, the subgroup may become a *splinter group*, which separates and forms a new organization. This process accounts for the many and varied Christian religious organizations which hold similar basic beliefs but have strong disagreements about the particular methods and means of transmitting them to others.

Implicit or abstractly embedded values (such as enhancement of the species) are seldom stated directly. Even more specific and concrete values (for example, economic gain, pleasure, self-expression, or service to others) often are not explicitly stated within organizations with long institutionalized histories. Whether abstract or concrete, explicit or implicit, they form the foundation for the functions of organizations and individuals within each human system.

Organizations and individuals who have agreed and made explicit their governing core values are more likely to create functional systems because individuals behave from agreed-upon common ground. Holding a common base of core governing values increases the likelihood that a shared vision will be held by members of an organization, that a clear mission can be stated, and that common goals can be established. Coherence in values, vision, mission, and goals makes possible coherent plans with measurable objectives, effective strategies, and meaningful evaluation. Organizations will develop coherent plans and be more efficient in accomplishing their goals when they can come to a consensus on values and a focused vision of the future.

School and Community Values. To be coherent and systematic, strategic planning must begin with an explanation of the core values contained in the organizational unit. In addition, those values must be compatible with the larger community's and with the cultural context surrounding the organization or institution. In planning school counseling programs, the professional core values must be consistent with the core values of the local school and community to attain and retain credibility.

Planning must rest on core values that have been articulated and made explicit by counselors and members of both the institution and the community. A congruent and coherent planning process begins with determining the core values within a system or a subsystem so that all components will be able to function from the beginning with a common, agreed-upon starting place. Having a set of core values that have been articulated through a process of consensus building offers the best possibility for a functional organization that has integrity, strength, and clarity about "where we are coming from" and "where we are going." Counselors, schools, and communities that intend to create a shared vision of the future must reach consensus on, and articulate clearly, the core governing values upon which their vision of the future is based.

Core Community Values. Core values in a community are those held by the population within the service area of the school. Public schools usually are accountable to layers of values found in the local community, in the state, and sometimes in the nation. Private or parochial schools usually start with a publicly held perception or a written expression of core values. Families choose the school because of some congruence between their own values and those presented by the sponsors or creators of the school.

A counselor can come to understand the core values of a community in at least two ways.

1. The first way—which is cumbersome and less practical—is to examine documents of various organizations within the community, such as these:

   • Chambers of commerce hold a particular set of values about economic growth and development.

   • Governmental officials may have policy statements that reflect the values of the community.

   • Churches, youth organizations, police, and civic groups usually distribute materials that reflect their values.

   • Documents outlining policies, procedures, rules, and regulations serve as indicators of significant values in the community. Clearly, governing values are woven into the fabric of every community, and common threads are found in the civic, religious, and private organizations in each.

2. A more efficient way to discover a community's core values is to assemble a representative *focus group* for the express purpose of discussing community values. (Particular techniques for reaching consensus on core values are discussed in chapter 7.)

Determining the community's core values is important because they are the basis from which the community sets priorities and perpetuates itself. Any successful educational activity, including the school itself, will find solid support from a community if members feel comfortable that the governing values of the school support the values of the community.

Core School Values.   A school's core values can be determined in the same way you find a community's values.

1. The most obvious documents to start with are those developed by the school board or other governing body. Many schools have written vision and mission statements. Board policies and other published information documents may contain philosophy or purpose statements and vision and mission statements as well as goals for the school. When only goal statements exist, some implicit values may be interpreted. For example, the priority goals may indicate some relative positioning in the value hierarchy for curriculum, faculty, physical plant, student services, safety, and community involvement.

2. Conversations with school board members, central office administrators, principals, and teachers often will indicate directly or indirectly their value positions.

3. If the school has not adopted written belief or vision statements, you may have to elicit a statement of core values by working with a focus group of educators. (Several techniques for reaching consensus on governing values within a school are discussed in chapter 7.)

Core School Counseling Values. Governing values within the counseling profession, as well as those held by the counseling staff in a school, are no less important than school and community values. Counselors work more effectively together and understand each other better when core values are explicitly shared and published. The process of writing down the core values of the professional counseling staff often is an enlightening experience. Typically professional counselors find many areas of agreement. When differences do exist, however, it is necessary for the counselors within a district or building to work together to reach consensus and then to publish their core values.

For example, if one counselor holds as a governing value "education is for creating a meaningful life," and another counselor values "education as preparation for work," the mission of the counseling program may be ambiguous. An appropriate procedure would be to clarify those differences so that both can say, "Our common value base is this: Education helps individuals with preparation for the future." At first glance, the difference may not be apparent. However, starting with either of the first two statements makes it possible to create quite different visions of the counseling program's future, while the third statement permits both governing values to peacefully coexist within a wide yet focused vision for the counseling program. Many of the arguments we school counselors have among ourselves are based on our failures to acknowledge and discuss the core values from which we are speaking.

VISION

Transforming Values into Vision

Until we arrive at a consensus on the core values of our profession, we will have little success in creating a shared vision of the future.

Professional School Counseling Vision. It remains to be seen whether the profession of school counseling can arrive at a consensus on its core values. However, each group of counselors functioning within a school system must articulate their own values, and make clear that these values are compatible with those of their community, so that strategic planning can proceed.

Community and School Vision. A community's vision of its own future—whether implied or discussed directly—is evident in the goals, plans, and actions of the various institutions, organizations, and groups within it. The current vision of a community may be discovered by asking individuals from various segments, "What is your view of this community?" And, "What do you see in the future for this community?" Or, "If you could imagine the perfect future for this community, what would you imagine?"

Generally the response will be somewhat individual; however, the responses from several knowledgeable community members may reveal a common thread of vision. If none is found, you may suspect that little agreement on a vision for the future has been achieved. The lack of a shared vision within a community may offer a leadership opportunity for the school. Or it may signal past difficulties which fragmented the community and are yet unresolved.

Achieving a functional community or school is difficult without a shared vision. Events may arise that drastically affect the future and that seem out of the control of community members. However, when a community has a picture of its future, its chances of surviving significant changes—whether brought by nature, the economy, or demographic shifts—will be higher. In other words, a community is better able to find new opportunities after a crisis if its members have a shared vision of the future.

Creating a vision of the future within a community can foster cohesion and involvement and release creative energy. For example, organized charities are more successful within a community when its members have a shared vision of how to serve various charity needs. Chambers of commerce are more successful in attracting new businesses and industries to developing communities when there is a shared vision of the economic future. Schools have more successful band, athletic, and building programs when the community and the school share a vision of the future.

In almost all communities, even those heavily populated with retired persons, nearly everyone is concerned with the quality of the schools. Given the fact that schools work with the children who represent the future of the community, it is essential that the schools and the community share a vision of the future. When schools and communities share such a vision, each component of a school can be developed to support the vision.

Shared Program Vision. Counseling programs are more widely understood and supported by the school and the community when there is a shared vision of who the counselors are and what they do to support the school/community vision. Creating a vision of your school's counseling program is best achieved when all stakeholders participate. Visions of the future vary according to community size, location, and community core values. For example, a suburban community of commuters to high-tech professional jobs in the city will certainly establish a different vision of the counseling program than will a rural community with few jobs. Whether the vision of the future supports maintenance of the status quo or change, it will suggest the mission for the school and reflect the governing core values of the community.

Chapter 4

GETTING STARTED

Reaching consensus among counseling staff can improve the chances for overall success and involvement. A key factor in the success of a planning effort is the active involvement of a majority of the counselors in the system. Without at least tacit approval of the majority, little district- or system-wide planning can occur.

The majority of counselors in one district we know of became motivated to begin the process after the superintendent endorsed the idea and advocated for the process to the entire counseling staff. Clearly, having administrative support from the beginning can provide encouragement. Still, if there is little collective interest in change, an individual counselor in a single school may begin planning. Of course, having the interest and involvement of all counselors in the school system will result in a better plan. But planning within a single building or at a particular level (elementary, junior high, or high school) may be the only approach possible when prospects for a district-wide effort are not good.

Beyond improving benefits for the entire district, working as a team increases the cohesiveness of the counseling staff and shows the school community the importance of collaborative planning.

Nonetheless, one counselor working alone in a single school can begin a team-centered, site-based planning process like the one described here and thereby demonstrate the advantages of systematic planning. (See "Examples from the Field" in chapter 10.)

SCHOOL BOARD AND ADMINISTRATION APPROVAL

Once the counselors have agreed to proceed with the planning process, you need a written proposal for administrative consideration and endorsement. A formal proposal is important because it involves the administration in the planning process, creates awareness of the direction the counseling program is taking, and provides a concrete guide for communicating with the school board and the community. If you want to ensure their support, you must get official sanction from the administrative staff and the board.

In addition to formalizing administrative support, getting approval of the plan signals everyone that the counseling staff is taking a proactive stance to improve services. Once the proposal has been completed, the staff should request that the school board endorse the plan at a regular board meeting. Once the board has endorsed the plan, fewer people will question the legitimacy of the counselors' planning efforts. With board endorsement, building principals and central office administrators are more likely to encourage and support planning meetings and other activities.

CONTENTS OF PROPOSAL

At a minimum, the proposal should include the following detailed and specific information.

What Is Going to Be Done?

The proposal should describe the broad aims of the planning effort, the major purposes for improving the counseling program, and the expected economy of effort. It should emphasize creating the highest level of quality possible through continuing improvement and redirection as the demographics of the student body and the community change.

Who Is Going to Be Involved?

The proposal should describe the categories of membership on the advisory team. Prior to completing this section, the counseling staff should consider the organizational structure and size of the district, whether or not there will be a steering committee (such a committee may be needed in large districts), how the advisory team will interact with other committees and teams in the district, and any other special factors.

How Will It Be Organized?

This section should describe in broad terms the responsibilities of the professional staff and members of the advisory team, including training, conducting needs assessments, setting goals, planning strategies, and evaluation. You also should spell out how evaluation data will be incorporated into ongoing revisions.

When Will the Process Begin?

This section should project a timeline for completion of the planning process. You should emphasize that the start-up of an effective process does not mean the end of the effort. Each planning cycle will simply lead to evaluation data, which then become the basis for redirection, update, and fine-tuning.

How Long Will It Take?

Somewhere in the proposal, you should predict when a document will be available for review and approval of the school board. You also should estimate the date by which the plan will be completed.

What Will Be the Impact of the Resulting Plan?

Be sure to give careful attention to the expected benefits of the planning process. Do not just emphasize specific outcomes, such as reduced dropout rates, absenteeism, and disciplinary problems. While these outcomes might be expected, you should emphasize in the proposal the benefits to counselors, teachers, students, parents, administrators, and community members. A clearly defined and articulated design for the counseling program will lead to broad-based understanding and support. You should include here the various components of the completed plan (e.g., organizational structure, budget, and professional development), and how other special efforts and programs already in place will be included. Showing how related functions will be incorporated into the plan demonstrates *economy of effort.*

Finally, you must present the completed proposal *through the appropriate channels for administrative endorsement.* With administrative endorsement, the counseling program will have a much-needed ally when the proposal finally goes before the school board for consideration. Administrative support also increases your chance of gaining full support from the school board, and a school board endorsement in turn validates the importance of the counseling program to the community. Board endorsement publicly says to the community *why* a counseling program is needed and emphasizes that the services provided by the counseling program are important to long-term school improvement. Figures 4.1 and 4.2 show a cover letter and a sample proposal for administrative approval.

THE ADVISORY TEAM

One of your first tasks is putting together a counseling program advisory team. This team is appointed by the board and consists of students, parents, teachers, administrators, the school board, and others from the community (e.g., ministers, mental health professionals, business persons, law enforcement officers, and government officials). The advisory team provides input to the counseling and administrative staff and serves as a link to the community. The team will be involved in planning, implementing, and evaluating the counseling program. (See chapter 3 for more information on advisory teams.)

SAMPLE OF A COVER MEMO

Date: Today's date
To: Superintendent of schools
From: Counseling staff
Subject: Proposal for long-term counseling program development

The attached proposal is submitted by the counseling staff. We seek your assistance in placing this proposal on the agenda for the next Board of Education meeting. The proposal provides a rationale and justification for a long-term planning and development project that will result in a complete upgrade of the services provided by the counselors in our district. Our aim is to foster a continuous improvement effort that is carried out under the oversight of a community, school administration, faculty, student, and the professional counseling team. Approval and sanction of this proposal is sought from the Board.

As you will note in the proposal, final selection and appointment of the advisory team will be requested at the next regular Board meeting following the Board's approval of the planning project. Once the advisory team has completed its work, the plan will be brought back to the Board for final review and adoption. Once final Board approval is granted, the plan will serve as the official document and guide for the delivery of professional counseling and guidance services in our schools.

If you have any questions about this proposal, please contact us. Your support to this point is most appreciated, and we look forward to attending the Board meeting so that we may answer any questions you or members of the Board may have.

Figure 4.1. Cover memo to accompany a long-term proposal: A sample.

SAMPLE PROPOSAL FOR
LONG-TERM IMPROVEMENT

Counselors in our district believe our schools exist for the purpose of transmitting the culture, knowledge, and skills required to preserve and enhance our way of life. We further believe the development of all students to the highest levels of learning possible, so that they are prepared to function successfully in a democratic society, is central to the mission of our school. We believe all students have the right to learn to read, to write, and to do mathematics. In addition, we believe they have a right to learn to communicate with peers and adults, to value themselves and others, to accept responsibility for their own behavior, to solve problems, to listen to others in a respectful manner, and to make wise decisions that do not harm themselves or others.

Students frequently are faced with increasingly challenging situations that require them to make wise decisions, solve problems, and assume responsibility for their behavior. The issues faced by children today are often much more difficult than those faced by previous generations. Children need ample opportunity to learn to manage their own behavior in a manner that is congruent with and acceptable in our community and the larger society. Youth also benefit from systematic opportunities to prepare for a future very different from the one their parents faced. Since we believe our children are our most precious resources, it is important that our school provide ample opportunity, appropriate facilitation, and adequate support for all students to grow and develop as well as to gain the skills and understanding needed to make wise and responsible choices. Our purposes as a community are better served when students have opportunities to learn to function appropriately in groups and sustain the intellectual habits they need to continue learning throughout their lives.

To this end, we propose a planning process that will result in a comprehensive developmental counseling program. We believe that a planned, sequential program including all grades from kindergarten through grade 12 will provide students with the most opportunities to develop in a manner consistent with their greatest potential.

Much as sequential curricular programs in mathematics are necessary for optimum learning of concepts and skills in that subject, sequential comprehensive curricular programs that foster learning about self and others in the context of life development are essential to maximum personal and social growth and development. We think students will be better equipped for making necessary decisions—from choosing postsecondary education to making personal decisions about responsible behavior in relationships with others—if they have a strong base of knowledge about themselves. Further, we think a well-designed data-driven and community-based program of planned and evaluated services is the best assurance that all aspects of maximum student learning, growth, and development have been attended to in our counseling program.

This proposal describes the process and the major steps we will pursue in creating a continuous planning mechanism in our school and community, through which we can consistently pursue the goal of providing the best possible services to our school and community.

Figure 4.2. Proposal for long-term program development: A sample.

The counseling and administrative staff should compile a list of prospective advisory team members. Once prospective members have been identified and have tentatively agreed to serve on the committee, the list should be presented to the school board for official approval and appointment.

PREPARING YOUR TEAM

The counselors should provide training workshops for the advisory team members, covering such topics as the team's purpose, function, and structure; professional competencies, training, and credentials of the counselors; types of situations for which the counselors have been trained; the beliefs, vision, and mission of the counseling program; and the specific tasks and assignments of the team.

DEVELOPING A TIMELINE

Completely implementing the program takes a commitment of five to six years. The first year will be devoted to

1. preparing and organizing the advisory team into a working group;

2. reviewing and refining the beliefs, vision, and mission of the counseling program;

3. conducting a needs assessment among students, parents, and school personnel;

4. identifying high-priority needs;

5. establishing counseling program goals;

6. writing objectives; and

7. helping the counseling staff develop activities to address identified needs.

Finally, having a well-developed and easily usable timeline, such as the one presented in Figure 4.3, is essential to completing strategic planning tasks.

SAMPLE TIMELINE FOR THE COMPLETION OF STRATEGIC PLANNING TASKS

Steps to Complete	Completion Date
School Board approval of the proposed planning process	Aug. 31 Year 1
Identification of persons who are willing to serve on the advisory team	Sept. 1 Year 1
School Board appointment of advisory team members	Sept. 30 Year 1
Complete the organization and training of the advisory committee	Oct. 31 Year 1
Development of refined beliefs, vision, and mission	Nov. 30 Year 1
Selection of needs assessment instruments	Dec. 20 Year 1
Printing and distribution of needs assessment surveys	Feb. 1 Year 1
Compilation of needs data	March 31 Year 1
Prioritized needs	April 10 Year 1
Development of written program goals	April 15 Year 1
Board approval of the complete written plan	July 15 Year 1
Implementation, monitoring, evaluation, and revision	End of Year 2
Implementation, monitoring, evaluation, and revision	End of Year 3
Implementation, monitoring, evaluation, and revision	End of Year 4
Implementation, monitoring, evaluation, and revision	End of Year 5
Begin major replanning cycle	End of Year 5
Conduct needs assessment	End of Year 5
Develop a new written plan	End of Year 6

Figure 4.3. Timeline for completion of strategic planning tasks: A sample.

Chapter 5

THE ADVISORY TEAM

Once you have secured administrative support and the school board has approved the planning proposal, the next step is to put together an advisory team. The advisory team will assist the counseling and administrative staff in planning, implementing, and evaluating the comprehensive K–12 counseling program. The team will become a central part of the support system in the community, serving as a link between various segments of the community and administrators, faculty, students, and groups who are served by the counseling staff.

The counseling staff must first decide the number of people who will serve on the team, the make-up of the team, and the best way to select members. Counselors new to the school system and those who have lived and served in the community for many years will provide differing views, and both can make important contributions in the decision-making process. Counselors who have been in the community for several years will know more about the official and unofficial sources of influence, who the decision makers are, and how separate parts of the community work (or do not work) together. Counselors new to the system are freer to think about ideals without any preconceptions of known persons and stereotypes. You should take care to discuss all views on the best design for the most workable advisory team.

STRUCTURAL CONSIDERATIONS

Size

The size of the advisory team will depend on the size of the school district. The team should be large enough to provide effective implementation and evaluation of the program, yet small enough to work cohesively. Committees in large districts can be organized into working subcommittees representing elementary, middle school/junior high, and secondary schools. In the largest districts, further division by building may be more effective, or a district-wide steering committee could be formed to coordinate and facilitate the work of various subcommittees. Small districts, however, may choose to function with one team composed of representatives from each of the three levels.

You need to consider the unique concerns of the district, total size, previous methods for organizing district-wide efforts, and ways of representing various interest groups or stakeholders. Once the advisory team is selected—even if it is a large team and will be divided into subgroups—it should meet as a total group during training and the initial planning sessions. Whether the advisory team functions as one working unit or as a unit of working subcommittees, you should continue to emphasize how the components fit together to ensure the continuity needed in the final plan. Keep before all team members the final goal, which is to ensure that all students have access to the full compliment of services needed.

Membership

The advisory team is a representative body of students, staff, parents, employers, and community leaders. For better communication and representation from all areas, the team should include teachers and parents from each building level, students from junior and senior high schools, an administrator from each level, a school board member, and some community members. You can look for community members from groups such as civic organizations, parent-teacher organizations, groups concerned with youth issues, business and industry associations, and city or county government.

It should go without saying that *the best teams are those with the most diversity.* A team with diversity in professional and community roles, gender, ethnicity, socioeconomic status, age, and life experiences ensures a strong and stable final product.

You should also try to include on the team one or more of the most critical opponents of the counseling program. For example, if a group in your community is opposed to certain views on self-esteem or group work, you should try to identify a leader of the group and recruit him or her as a member of the team. Our experience with districts caught in a destructive cycle of reactionary and inappropriate communication suggests that including representatives from faction groups from the beginning goes a long way toward building mutual respect and cooperation. Chances are good that you will find school board support for such an appointment. Many faction groups have worked to elect school board representatives in the past few years and have been successful in building strong coalitions around conservative values.

Strengthening school counseling is best accomplished when respect is shown toward *all* community groups, when *all* groups are included and valued in the process. If we want community support, we must educate all of the community about the purposes and strategies of school counseling. We must open ourselves to collaboration with persons and groups who have differing world views and diverse value systems if we expect to reach understanding and, more importantly, model the very heart of our beliefs about counseling.

Choosing Your Team

Final selection of advisory team members should be a joint effort between counselors and administrators. You should seek nominations from teachers and other school system professionals and community members, then compile a list of potential team members. Possible appointees should be willing to commit to considerable time and effort during the early stages of program development and to continued involvement throughout their term of service on the team.

Individual team members should be appointed for a minimum one-year term to ensure cohesiveness and continuity in team efforts. Procedures vary from district to district, but most decide to begin with staggered terms so that only a small percentage of new members begin during any one year. Rotating committee members after one year helps alleviate lengthy terms of commitment and allows for participation by a variety of representatives from the community.

Once the final list of potential team members has been completed, each member should be officially appointed by the school board and notified via formal letter. This process offers the opportunity for publicity in local media. Informing the community about the purpose of the advisory team increases community participation and establishes increased visibility for the team's work.

Figure 5.1 is a sample proposed list of advisory team members. It illustrates the breadth of representation.

Forming and Organizing the Team

Usually, one person is designated to initiate formation of the advisory team. Larger districts that have a central office director of counseling or a director of pupil personnel can assign that individual to perform this task. Schools that do not have a designated leader for the counseling program can appoint one counselor to begin the formation process and to serve as the contact between the advisory team and the professional staff. Small districts that have only one counselor should simply have the counselor and a designated administrator collaborate in forming the advisory team.

The designated leader is responsible for contacting the appointed team members and verifying their willingness to accept

SAMPLE LIST OF PROPOSED
ADVISORY TEAM MEMBERS

Memo

To: Superintendent

From: Counseling staff

Subject: Counseling program proposed advisory team members

The following individuals are recommended for appointment to the *Counseling Program Advisory Team*. We welcome your comments and are willing to assist in any way we can. If this list meets with your approval, please place these names in nomination for board appointment at the next school board meeting.

Name	Representative	Years of Appointment
Linda Listener	Senior High Counselor & Coordinator of the Advisory Committee	–
Bill Career	Senior high counselor	3
Jane Helper	Junior high counselor	2
John I. Care	Junior high counselor	1
Jill Loving	Elementary counselor	3
Jerry Duso	Elementary counselor	2
Patty Hugmore	Elementary counselor	1
Hugh Commander	Senior high asst. principal	3
Sally Principal	Junior high principal	3
Jim Finder	Elementary principal	3
Willa Weschsler	School psychologist	2
Donna Doright	Senior high student	1
Johnny Smart	Junior high student	2
Paula Pillar	Elementary student	1
Edna Educator	Senior high teacher	3
Barry Good	Junior high teacher	2

Polly Pointer	Fifth-grade teacher	1
Mary Printer	Second-grade teacher	3
Ralph Respect	Senior high parent	2
Amanda Teen	Junior high parent	1
Molly Mother	Elementary parent	3
Holly Hypo	Nurse	2
Bud Business	Chamber of Commerce rep.	1
Phil Upchurch	Minister	3
John Doe	School board member	2
Doris Merchant	Business owner	1
John Justice	Police officer	3
Carrie Forth	Mental health agency director	2
Steven Still	Funeral home director	1

Figure 5.1. Proposed list of advisory team members: A sample.

appointment to the team. If notification is by written correspondence, the letter should include congratulations, an expression of thanks from the counseling staff for the person's willingness to serve, and a list of possible dates for the first meeting (see Figure 5.2). It is helpful to include a brief form with a signature space that acknowledges the appointee's intention to serve (see Figure 5.3). The form also can include spaces for telephone numbers, current address, and preferred dates and times for the first meeting.

Training the Team

Once the advisory team has been appointed, you should immediately begin a series of training and planning sessions. The counseling staff plans the training and should participate as workshop leaders for various segments of the training sessions. Training sessions should be well-planned, efficiently managed, and comprehensive. Be sure to schedule the sessions at times when all members can attend. All sessions should be lively, informative, and provide for member participation.

SAMPLE LETTER TO TEAM APPOINTEES

Dear Mr./Mrs.

Congratulations on your appointment to the Mill Creek Counseling Program Advisory Team. I am excited about having your assistance with our counseling program, and want to thank you for your willingness to serve as a member of our district advisory team.

Providing a comprehensive K–12 program is a high priority for our counseling and administrative staff. We know your input will be beneficial to our programming efforts. Input from parents, students, educators, and business representatives is vital to the long-term success of our program.

We look forward to working with you and are planning now to schedule the first meeting of the advisory team at a time convenient for all members.

The attached form will serve to verify your acceptance of this appointment. Please provide the information requested and return this form as quickly as possible. You will be contacted soon regarding an appropriate date for our first meeting. At this initial meeting, we will discuss the advisory team's purpose and role in developing a revised district-wide counseling program as well as begin training and preparation for your work. Prior to beginning the actual work of the team, we will provide extensive support and preparation to all team members.

Thank you again for your interest in service to our students. If you have any questions, please do not hesitate to call me at 555-0000.

Cordially yours,

Linda Listener, Convener (or other title)
Counseling Program Advisory Team

Figure 5.2. Letter for appointees to advisory team: A sample.

ACCEPTANCE AND VERIFICATION FORM

Yes, I will serve on the Counseling Advisory Team.

Name:_____
(Signature)

Address: _____

_____

Business phone:_____

Home phone:_____

Suggested meeting time (please circle)

Mon.   Tues.   Wed.   Thurs.   Fri.   Weekend

A.M.   P.M.

Figure 5.3. Postcard sent with letter to each appointee to advisory team: A sample.

Training sessions can be structured in a number of ways, but we recommend no fewer than three workshops, each running three hours. Our experience conducting such workshops suggests that a three-hour session each week for three weeks is sufficient to inform members and reach the beginnings of a working team atmosphere. An agenda, including suggested activities and a discussion of group responsibilities, is included later in this chapter to help you design your training workshop.

The team training process is absolutely critical to the success of counseling program planning and development. Counselors must be prepared to present information in a coherent and informative manner. *Organization is the key to effective training efforts.* What follow here are some suggestions for conducting advisory team training sessions.

You should have relevant material available for members at each meeting. For example, you could prepare in advance a three-ring binder for each team member. Possible handouts include belief, vision, and mission statements for the school and the counseling program; data on the school population; statistics on youth or employment from the community; standards for preparing school counselors; copies of American School Counselors Association journals or newsletters; and the Code of Ethics for School Counselors. Providing such information at the beginning demonstrates the professional status of school counseling to the team. Team members can refer to information in the binder throughout their terms of service and supply others in the community with essential information.

A well-informed advisory team allows all team members to bring their personal and professional resources to the task at hand. Unless team members are well-prepared, much time will be wasted in irrelevant discussion and false starts. When too many wasted motions and delays occur, absenteeism and discouragement increase. The efforts of the counseling staff to invite, understand, and value team member contributions are essential.

The counseling staff should meet regularly to update those counselors who are not serving as members of the team. All the counseling staff should regularly and promptly receive current information and summaries of meetings. Counselors not directly involved may experience anxiety about what decisions are being made and will benefit from concrete updates. Reducing anxiety about the decisions being made helps ensure that each member of the counseling staff remains supportive and available as a resource to the team members as their work proceeds. Regular meetings with the full counseling staff help to keep down rumors and maintain an accurate record of the team's work. Minutes of each team meeting should be distributed to counselors and administrators, so that if significant questions arise, they can be brought back to the team for discussion. Systematic efforts should be made by all counselors to sustain a positive, proactive position in regard to the team's work. When mechanisms are planned from the beginning for providing feedback and information, misunderstandings can be minimized.

Producing a final working plan for strengthening the school's counseling program depends on several factors. Of primary importance is forming an appropriate and strong advisory team. Doing so legitimizes the team's work. No less important is preparing the team well and ensuring adequate support from both counselors and administrators. Once these two aspects of the advisory team are in place, the construction of a support system can begin.

ADVISORY TEAM WORKSHOP

Session One

The first workshop session can determine the degree of productivity of the team. First impressions are critical when volunteers meet as part of a task group. Much of the success of the planning process (as well as the significance and usefulness of the final product) is signaled within a few minutes of the group's formation.

Diversity and previous relationships between members of the team (or lack thereof) should be considered when you are planning the first meeting. You must prepare the first training session carefully. Pay particular attention to planning several team-building activities. Careful structuring of both the group atmosphere and team building along with the task and content portions of the session will improve the chances that the team will function effectively.

You should be sure the layout of the room is conducive to interaction during the get-acquainted part of the session. Appropriate refreshments, nonthreatening member introductions, and warm-up exercises should be carefully planned. If possible, the informal get-acquainted and refreshment time should be held in a different space from the more formal part of the session. A room large enough to accommodate both functions is ideal. Arranging tables in a circle, with name tags visible to everyone and already in place, signals that each person is valuable. Try to distribute any well-known persons throughout the group. A three-ring binder with all handouts needed for the session, personalized for each team member, should be prepared in advance and placed at each person's seat.

Session One should set the tone for productive working time in an enjoyable and meaningful atmosphere in which differing views are welcomed and everyone has an important contribution to make. This session should be at the least two hours long and address the following goals:

1. Develop cohesiveness among members

2. Discuss the purposes of the advisory committee

3. Outline the committee's functions and contributions

Content to Cover in Session One. The advisory team will perform a sequence of functions throughout the planning, implementation, and evaluation phases of the counseling program. The planning cycle is often thought of as occurring in three phases.

Phase I: Build a Foundation. This is the most demanding phase of the planning cycle. Many people involved in planning consider the tasks completed in this phase to *be* planning. The process described here, however, considers these tasks as only the first part of the planning cycle. Clearly, the bulk of time and energy is invested in this phase. The full impact of the investment during Phase I becomes apparent only after two or three years of implementation and further adjustments. Advisory teams who are able to complete Phase I will find the demands lessened drastically with more opportunity for observing the effects of the work they completed.

Phase I advisory team tasks are listed below:

1. The early contributions of the advisory team are critical. Prior to appointment of the team, counselors should have

developed a set of core beliefs, a mission statement, and a vision for the counseling program. The first part of the planning process is to make certain that the foundation of the planning effort—as reflected in the belief, mission, and vision statements—is strong, clear, and shared. The advisory team is invited to review, refine, and adopt these statements as the base of operations from which all other steps in the planning process will arise. Once the final statements have been polished and agreed upon, the advisory team can achieve consensus on decisions, because each new decision will be directed by the beliefs, mission, and vision set forth.

2. The next task is to plan for an assessment of student, teacher, parent, and administrator needs. Options for needs assessment are outlined and sample instruments are available in chapter 7.

3. The third task in the planning sequence is establishing program goals. The advisory team should establish goals for the counseling program and write those goals to reflect the highest priority needs, as identified in the needs assessment. Once goals have been selected, the advisory team will assist the counseling staff in deciding which strategies and activities will be most effective in achieving the program goals.

4. The next task is building a set of management and outcome objectives that will ensure persistent and continuous progress toward the goals. Once objectives have been constructed, the basic framework for the program will be in place. Well-constructed management objectives include what is to be done, when, by whom, and what record will be made to show that each event did, in fact, occur. Clear, well-written management objectives make accountability for counselors and others a simple matter of reviewing the evidence. Well-constructed outcome objectives show the expected result of each activity and indicate how the result will be measured.

5. The fifth and final task in the first phase of the planning cycle is to formally approve the final plan and recommend the K–12 counseling program plan to the administrative staff and the board. Board approval of the completed plan will ensure the continuation of a coherent effort even when there are changes in counseling staff or administrative leadership in the district.

The accomplishments of the advisory team should be communicated to the larger community on a regular basis. You should designate a publicity person to write brief progress reports to the school board and the local media. The advisory team's efforts to strengthen the aims, focus, and results of the counseling program can enhance public relations and make visible the important work of the counselors. Individual team members can make important contributions by contacting persons who have access to resources for special projects and by helping with activities coordinated by counselors, such as career and college days.

Phase II: Implement and Monitor. The second phase of program planning begins with the advisory team's completion of an annual evaluation. We recommend this evaluation be used to monitor and make adjustments in the program's operation. The annual evaluation serves to set markers of progress toward the stated goals, which are the destinations for the five- or six-year plan.

Phase III: Evaluate and Replan. The third phase in the planning cycle is the completion of a systematic and comprehensive evaluation of all aspects of the program including personnel, administrative support, operation, goal attainment, and needs assessment. The third phase results in a major improved and revised plan for School Board approval.

Session Two

In Session Two of the advisory team training, you should provide background information on the profession of school counseling; the school district's beliefs, vision, and mission; and the beliefs and values of the professional counselors. You also should introduce the vision and mission of the counseling program.

Goal 1 for Session Two: Inform and Educate Members. Topics and time during the second session should be shared by all members of the counseling staff. This way, members of the advisory team get to know members of the counseling staff. Counselors may choose the segments they want to lead and should lead the portions that display their strengths. Recommended topics include, but are not limited to

- preparation and training of school counselors,

- certification requirements for the counseling staff, and

- specific counseling skills, experience, and expertise of counselors in the district.

You should tell the advisory team about counselor preparation, certification, and specific skills. A lack of knowledge about what services the counseling staff is qualified for and can deliver could result in team decisions that fail to build on the greatest strengths of the professional counseling staff.

Topic 1: Background Information on Professional Counseling. The counselor of the 1960s was primarily a career specialist who helped students find work and plan for further education. Counselors today engage in actual counseling activities as well as impart knowledge. You can discuss the information here during the training session or simply summarize it in a handout given to each advisory team member. Keep in mind that Council on Accreditation of Counseling and Related Education Programs (CACREP) standards currently are being rewritten and will likely undergo changes within the next four years. You can get current recommendations for your team training from CACREP. If the team is to support the counseling program and communicate with the community about the services available to students and parents, members must be aware of the following information.

Counselor preparation and training. Most counselor training programs include a core of courses required by CRACEP (1988). Many also require courses that prepare counselors for the unique needs and demands of the clientele in the work setting. Additionally, universities and colleges often coordinate course work with state departments of education in individual states and regions. Training programs enhance counselor knowledge and competency in the following areas:

1. *Human growth and development:* The counselor understands the nature and needs of individuals at all developmental levels, with an understanding of psychological, sociological, and physiological development. Understandings of human behavior (normal and abnormal), personality theory, and learning theories also are acquired during training.

2. *The helping relationship:* During graduate study each counselor develops a philosophical base as well as specific skills in creating helping relationships. This base emphasizes the development of the counselor/student relationship toward self-awareness and self-understanding.

3. *Consultation:* The counselor is trained in consultation with a variety of professionals. The counselor is aware of the importance of consultation to providing broad and effective services for students and their families.

4. *Counseling theory:* The counselor has formulated a personal theory that includes techniques appropriate for the age and developmental level of students. The counselor is aware of prominent counseling theories (TA, RET, reality, person-centered, Adlerian, behavioral, etc.). He or she can apply various approaches to unique situations, since each student is a unique individual with unique needs.

5. *Group counseling:* The counselor understands group theory, types of groups, group practices, methods, dynamics, and facilitating skills.

6. *Lifestyle and career development:* The counselor is knowledgeable about vocational choice theory, the relationship between career choice and lifestyle, sources of occupational and educational information, approaches to career decision making, and career development.

7. *Appraisal and measurement:* The counselor has developed a framework for understanding the individual, including methods of data gathering and interpretation; individual and group testing; case study approaches; the study of individual differences; and differences in ethnic, cultural, and gender factors in appraisal and measurement.

8. *Interpersonal relations:* The counselor has developed communication skills that help him or her relate effectively to students, teachers, parents, administrators, and people in the community.

9. *Curriculum development:* The counselor is knowledgeable about developing a curriculum that meets the needs of all students. He or she can help students select courses that will help them reach their educational goals, and is aware of trends that might necessitate adjusting the curriculum. The counselor helps administrators when a change in curriculum is indicated.

10. *Professional orientation:* The counselor participates in professional organizations, follows a code of ethics developed by the American Counseling Association and the American School Counselors Association (ASCA), is aware of legal considerations in working with minors, and is involved in continuing education programs required for certification and licensing.

11. *Crisis intervention:* The counselor is aware of the multitude of problems students may experience, is trained in identifying possible crisis situations, and is prepared

to deal with these situations if they arise. If the counselor does not feel the situation is within his or her area of expertise, he or she knows who and where to refer the student or family for additional in-depth counseling services.

12. *Program management:* The counselor knows about student, staff, family, and community needs. The counselor coordinates and administers a program that serves those needs.

The planning process is crucial if administrators, faculty, and the general public are to view the program as a vital, integral part of the school program. Several factors are involved in program management:

- Identifying needs via needs assessment instruments

- Setting goals and developing objectives

- Developing a time management system that allows the counselor to perform effectively

- Organizing the counseling staff, which helps ensure that all students are receiving needed information and assistance at all grade levels

- Developing methods to ensure open communication among counselors, teachers, administrators, students, and the community, which ultimately lead to support of the program

- Monitoring for effectiveness of counseling activities

- Evaluating the program through formal and informal evaluation tools and input from the advisory team, which brings about program improvement

Certification requirements. School counselor certification requirements vary from state to state. Your explanation of those requirements must be tailored to fit your individual situation. The following example was taken from the current Missouri State Department of Elementary and Secondary Education Counselor Certification Requirements:

The professional counselor certification is issued to persons who meet the following requirements:

1. A valid teaching certificate (elementary or secondary), as required to teach in the public schools of the state.

2. A minimum of two years of approved teaching experience. (About 25 states do not require teaching certification or experience.)

3. Completion of a master's degree with a major emphasis in elementary or secondary school counseling from a college or university meeting approval of the State Department of Education.

4. One year of accumulated paid employment (other than in teaching or counseling).

5. Recommendation for certification from the designated official of a college or university approved to prepare counselors (secondary or elementary) by the State Department of Education. Such recommendations and certifications are based upon the completion of a planned program including a minimum number of approved graduate credits in counseling courses, with a minimum number of hours focused on counseling in secondary or elementary schools.

6. Successful completion of at least three credit hours is required from the following core courses:

   a. Introduction to Personal and Professional Development in Counseling

   b. Foundations of Secondary or Elementary School Counseling

c. Individual and Group Appraisal

d. Life Span/Career Development

e. Theories and Techniques of Secondary or Elementary School Counseling

f. Theories and Techniques of Group Counseling

g. Practicum in Counseling

h. Internship in a secondary or elementary school setting

Topic 2: Counselor Skills. Counseling helps students develop self-understanding, self-acceptance, and self-direction. The counselor works with individuals, small groups, and classes. Students are counseled on emotional, physical, personal, and social problems, and on career development. The counselor can help students develop accurate self-concept; communication skills; conflict resolution and decision making skills; positive peer relations, family relationships, and other adult relationships; career awareness, exploration, and decision making; course selection and career planning; and personal issues, such as dating, human sexuality, substance abuse, depression, school phobias, loss of significant person, pregnancy, suicide, and adjusting to parental divorce.

Individual counseling. Students may be referred to the counselor by a teacher or parents, or they may seek assistance on their own. Students seek counseling for any of the reasons mentioned above.

Group counseling. In group counseling, the counselor can meet the needs of many students. Generally, counseling groups include students who share common concerns or problems. Within the group setting, students can develop communication and decision-making skills while receiving support from peers and the counselor. The potential for personal growth and social development is greatly enhanced by participating in a group, since students receive feedback from the counselor and peers in a secure, caring environment. Topics discussed in the group setting may include any of those mentioned above.

Family counseling. The school offers a safe, secure environment for the initial steps in family counseling. Parents may be more likely to seek help from the school counselor, since he or she works in an educational setting. The school counselor usually does not provide intensive family therapy. After working with the student and the parents, the counselor decides whether the family needs more intensive counseling and then refers the family to a community agency. If the counselor has developed a positive, trusting relationship with the family, the probability of the family following through with the counseling process is increased. After making a referral, with the permission of the family, the counselor may provide the family therapist with information on the student's school performance, peer relationships, and interventions that have been tried previously. In the later stages of the counseling process, the school counselor can help implement strategies that have been agreed upon in family counseling and support both the student and teachers in improving behavior at school and academic performance.

Guided classroom activities. Classroom activities generally are performed in cooperation with teachers. These are directed toward the personal, social, educational, and career development of all students. Classroom activities are basically informational in nature and focus on preventing future problems that may arise in the normal process of growth and development. Topics that may be addressed in the classroom setting include orientation for students new to the school system; understanding interests, skills, and personal characteristics; decision making, career planning, and goal setting; improving study habits; improving interpersonal communication skills; conflict resolution; making and keeping friends; drug and alcohol abuse and use; and human sexuality.

Consultation. The counselor's knowledge of student behavior can complement teacher efforts in identifying student needs; help create a more positive classroom climate; help in the development of experiences that emphasize self-understanding and enhance educational and career development; and help teachers, parents, and administrators understand the influence they exert on students (Keats, 1974). Consulting with significant adults implies an indirect service to students. It strengthens interventions and can prevent certain problem behaviors. The counselor can help teachers and parents understand student behavior that may be preventing educational and personal success. Besides parents and teachers, counselors also consult with administrators and health and community agency personnel.

Coordination. Within the school system and in the community, the counselor coordinates activities and contacts that enhance the development of the students. Within the school system, the counselor may direct and plan staff meetings aimed at enhancing the staff's understanding of student needs. The counselor provides leadership for the advisory team and often coordinates the involvement of resource persons in career education activities. The counselor is aware of community services—among them, psychological, social work, and health services—that can be used by the school. The counselor is sensitive to the need for and is knowledgeable of supportive services, and makes referrals whenever necessary for meeting student needs (Keats, 1974).

The counselor may also coordinate the school's assessment services. He or she is familiar with both group and individual assessment instruments. The counselor helps students, teachers, administrators, and parents understand the purposes and proper uses of tests. The counselor interprets results from assessment instruments to students, teachers, and parents. Results also are used to help students choose courses and set goals for the future.

Communication. A primary benefit of a successful program is the counselor's ability to communicate effectively with students and adults. In communicating with students, the counselor has a working knowledge of student language and media which, in turn, strengthens the student-counselor relationship of openness and trust (Keats, 1974). The counselor's ability to communicate effectively with teachers and administrators enhances the chances of a supportive network within the school system. With effective communication, teachers are more likely to feel comfortable seeking help from the counselor, and administrators may be more inclined to include the counselor in program planning. Effective communication with parents enables the counselor to encourage parents to become actively involved in their child's total development. Parents may attend student-teacher conferences more willingly, serve on parent advisory teams, and become involved in parent education programs.

Curriculum. A primary area of concern for the counselor is the emotional life of students. Since most school curricula are heavily concentrated on cognitive factors, the counselor can have a positive impact on the lives of students by integrating an affective aspect. The counselor can introduce teaching procedures and provide in-service programs that enable teachers to develop skills and materials for integrating affective and cognitive education. To establish this type of curriculum, the counselor provides clearly defined objectives and an organized method for evaluating student growth, assists teachers in developing effective interpersonal communication skills, and trains teachers to conduct guided classroom activities (Keats, 1974).

Goal 2 for Session Two: Inform Team Members of the Beliefs, Values, Vision, and Mission of the School and of the Counseling Program. The beliefs, values, vision, and mission of the school, as adopted by the school board, should be presented and discussed by the administrative staff. The counseling staff should follow with a presentation of the beliefs, values, vision, and mission of the counseling program. It is important during this presentation to emphasis that the advisory team will have an opportunity to revise and refine these statements. You should show the common agreements between school and counseling program statements.

Goal 3 for Session Two: Give an Overview of the Stages of Planning, Implementation, and Evaluation Work. You should emphasize long-term improvement of the total program through needs assessment, establishment of goals, implementation of program activities, and evaluation. The evolutionary nature of the planning, implementation, and evaluation cycle also should be emphasized. Noting the significant time investment required during the first phase and the significant decrease in time required after the first year is important during this training session.

Session Three

Goal for Session Three: Organize the Advisory Team. The primary aim of the third training session is to work out the details of organizing the team. You should provide time at the beginning to discuss possible alternative methods for organizing the team, but final decisions should be made by the advisory team itself. We recommend that the organization of the advisory team take place only after the team has selected a team leader or devised whatever means of operating it has chosen.

A number of decisions can be made during Session Three: The team can decide on the need for subcommittees, recorders, and other team roles as well as on meeting dates and frequency, lines of communication, and support resources. It is important to turn over the decision making of how and when the team will convene and function soon after beginning Session Three. Making it clear that the team has full responsibility for its own life will create some ambiguity in the beginning but will lead to a strong team and significant accomplishments in the long run.

Timelines for moving responsibility from the professional staff to the advisory team will vary based on the leadership and expertise among team members. It is important to turn over the responsibility as soon as possible without leaving the team adrift and unclear about its assignment. Some teams will need additional encouragement; this will become apparent as questions are asked repeatedly as a way of remaining dependent on the professional staff. Including one or more counselors who are skilled group facilitators on the team may help the team make the transition from trainees to self-directed team. Very dependent teams may need help identifying resources and establishing explicit task assignments and responsibilities for tasks such as telephone contacts and record keeping. Members of the counseling staff may serve as resource persons or ad hoc members of various subcommittees. Sometimes they may even have to serve as appointed or elected chairpersons of critical subcommittees. An agenda showing the date, time, and place should be mailed to each team member and various media contacts one week prior to each scheduled meeting. Other tips on holding effective meetings may be useful to less sophisticated teams.

Once the advisory team begins its work, the counseling staff will want to maintain contact with committee chairpersons, monitor progress toward completion of subcommittee tasks, and provide information needed by subcommittees. In larger districts a formal means of monitoring, supporting, and reporting to all counselors may be needed.

As members of the advisory team become informed about the counseling program and communicate their knowledge to other members of the community, a significant base of support will be created and maintained. The best public relations efforts are those that occur on a person-to-person level. Well-informed team members with support from counselors will be invaluable in conveying the significance and effectiveness of the counseling program.

Chapter 6

BUILDING THE FOUNDATION

The first part of this chapter shows how the initial components of a comprehensive plan form the foundation upon which other parts of the plan are built. The foundation of any system of services—whether delivered through an institution or by a group of individuals within a system—is a clear understanding of the system's identity and the fundamental core beliefs of the system. Core beliefs are the governing beliefs and values upon which decisions are based and actions are taken.

IDENTITY

Simply stated, identity answers these questions:

Who are we within this unit?

Who is considered part of this unit?

What constitutes the nature of our existence?

How does the makeup of this unit relate to the systemic context in which the unit functions?

Identity statements usually are simple and short and convey clearly the identity of the unit, individual, or organization. For example, the identity of the American School in Japan, as described in its 1994-95 self-study for the Western Association of Schools and Colleges, could be stated this way:

> **The American School in Japan:** An independent school operating for the benefit of expatriates temporarily living in Japan; binational families (e.g., Japanese/American); and Japanese families who have returned from living abroad. It selects excellent students each year who attend nursery through twelfth grades in Chofu-shi, Tokyo, Japan.

This example makes clear the who, where, and what of the American School in Japan.

Many organizations mistakenly assume that their identity is fully understood. The most successful organizations make clear to themselves and to others their identity. Having a clear identity statement helps focus the energies of all stakeholders in an organization. If an organization has a confused identity, members may be uncertain about their purposes and the tasks they are to perform. An organization stating its identity as "Your Local Long-Distance Phone Company" will have a very different view of its functions and its future than an organization identifying itself as, "Global Communications." Mottoes and logos often are attempts to convey identity. For example, a service organization working with homeless persons whose sign reads "Emergency Shelter" may focus its energies differently than one whose sign reads "Shelter for Now—Life Skills for Later."

It is important to determine and clearly state for public consumption the nature of your school or counseling program's identity. People's identities often are tied closely to their significant life roles. The identity of the school and counseling program is also tied to the significance of its role. In our Western culture, for example, we often ask about a person's work identity when we meet him or her for the first time. Typically, the question comes up within the first few minutes of a conversation. In fact, in some settings a person's name and work role are given together at the time of the introduction. Determining the nature of an individual's work provides a basis for conversation, assigning status, and, to some extent, the future of any social transactions.

Defining your identity allows stakeholders to judge whether or not benefits can be derived or needs can be met through further interaction with you. In much the same way, institutions and organizations interact with other institutions and organizations because of the nature of their identities the extent to which each can derive benefit from the other. Similarly, individuals want to know about an organization's identity prior to engaging in business or service transactions with the organization.

CORE BELIEFS AND GOVERNING VALUES

You should develop a statement of core beliefs and governing values before engaging in any further program development. It is the cornerstone on which the entire counseling program is built. A strong, clear statement of beliefs, which are compatible with the beliefs of the school, forms the foundation of a coherent program planning and management effort. The advisory team should direct its first efforts toward reviewing and refining the statement of beliefs and governing values developed by the counseling staff for the counseling program.

The advisory team's review should ensure that the counseling program's beliefs and governing values agree with the local school district's beliefs and governing values and also reflect the values and beliefs of the counseling staff. Community members of the team will want to consider the belief and value statements to ensure they can be supported by the larger community. The belief and governing values statements should reflect the counseling program's support to the educational programs of the school. Developing, refining, and adopting a statement of beliefs and governing values will give strength to the counseling program.

Most beliefs and values commonly held by educators are generally accepted among counseling professionals. Additionally, the counseling profession has a belief and value base from which counselors help students with personal and family issues, pressures from peers, decision making, celebrations of success, and changes or adjustments related to the normal process of human development. Core beliefs held by counselors and many other educators include the notion that all individuals have an inherent right to develop to their fullest potential. Therefore, the school community has an obligation to provide the appropriate learning opportunities and to assist individuals through enhancement of the normal developmental process.

To reach a consensus on a clear statement of core beliefs, consistent with the school's statement of beliefs and the basic tenants of the counseling profession, the advisory team must take time to discuss, explore, and refine the values, beliefs, and world views represented in the belief statements presented by the counselors. The team will want to make sure that these are compatible with those held by the community, as represented by community team members, to prevent conflict and disagreement later in the planning process. Conflicts over beliefs and values often are the most powerful kind and lie at the root of conflicts within many organizations. It is essential that beliefs and values are addressed from the very beginning in order to have a positive planning process. Sample statements of core beliefs are shown in Figures 6.1 and 6.2. These illustrate how the school's beliefs and beliefs in the counseling program are related.

The sample core belief statement in Figure 6.1 is rather long and resembles what a few years ago might have been called a *statement of philosophy*. One difficulty with having a long and elaborate statement is that not very many people will take the time to read it. A more effective approach might be an abbreviated version such as that shown in Figure 6.2.

The set of core beliefs and values listed in Figure 6.2 make explicit the commitments of the educational community. Having a common set of core beliefs like this makes clear which curricular

CORE BELIEFS STATEMENT
FROM SCHOOL DISTRICT A

Education is the process by which our youth acquire the knowledge and skills to function successfully in our democratic society. Successful functioning requires high levels of knowledge, the ability to solve problems, an openness to continued learning, and an understanding of the place of humankind in the ecology of the planet. Specific and significant opportunities that encompass the arts, development of physical skill, expertise in human communication and social interaction, as well as knowledge of self are essential to full individual functioning and preservation of the future of our democratic way of life. We believe our school is central to the education and preservation of our youth for a positive tomorrow.

We believe that each child is unique, with individual worth. Therefore, in our school we attempt to assure the acceptance of each child and provide opportunities to gain experiences and to enhance social, emotional, physical, and intellectual development. We believe education should help each child learn about him- or herself and learn the skills needed to engage in appropriate relationships with other persons.

We believe the purpose of education in this school district is the improvement of the knowledge, skills, attitudes, and understandings of each individual according to his or her developmental ability. One of the fundamental rights of every individual is the right of equal access to educational opportunity, regardless of race, creed, or socioeconomic status.

Figure 6.1. Core beliefs in statement format: A sample.

CORE BELIEFS AND VALUES OF THE
COUNSELING PROGRAM AT SCHOOL DISTRICT A

We believe:

All students must have opportunities to learn.

Education is the key to preserving our society and the future of humankind.

Intellectual, social, emotional, and physical learning are equally important.

Problem solving and thoughtful understanding of human matters are primary.

Each member of our educational community is essential to accomplishing our mission.

Adaptability to change will increasingly become a necessary basic skill.

Communicating and collaborating with others are primary to learning.

Figure 6.2. Core beliefs and governing values, stated as beliefs: A sample.

designs are to be emphasized as well as which ancillary services will be supported. If members of the educational community don't agree on the basic beliefs, conflict and competing efforts will fragment resources and the directions set forth will be pursued less systematically.

Contrast the list in Figure 6.2 with the core beliefs shown in Figure 6.3. Consider the conflicting values and beliefs and their implications for program planning and subsequent curricular experiences.

CORE BELIEFS AND VALUES
OF SCHOOL DISTRICT B

We Believe:

Students with the most ability should be rewarded with opportunity.

The future of humankind rests on attaining the highest level of basic skills.

While all students can learn, those who demonstrate high levels of motivation are most likely to benefit from the opportunities provided and should get more assistance.

Physical ability will be of less importance in the future than academic skills.

High expectations lead to high levels of performance.

Figure 6.3. Core beliefs and governing values of a school district, stated as beliefs: A sample.

Now consider another approach, reflected in the statement of core values from the International School of Kuala Lumpur in Malaysia (see Figure 6.4). The beliefs in this document contain some statements common to many schools around the world and others that reflect the unique setting of the Malaysian environment.

Figure 6.5 illustrates yet another approach to stating the core beliefs of a counseling program. This lengthy and detailed set of core beliefs may be acceptable as a working document for internal use. However, a briefer, more succinct statement of beliefs will communicate the program's identity more clearly to members of the advisory team and others.

(Continued on page 70.)

CORE BELIEFS AND VALUES OF THE INTERNATIONAL SCHOOL OF KUALA LUMPUR, MALAYSIA

We Believe:

Students are our *raison d'etre.*

Education is a partnership of parents, students, and the school.

All individuals should be treated with respect and dignity.

Physical, mental, and emotional well-being are important for all students.

Personal accountability for high standards of behavior—including trust, honesty, and integrity—are important for all students.

We should provide continuous open and honest communication.

It is imperative to attract, motivate, and retain outstanding faculty and staff.

Our cultural diversity and the Malaysian environment enrich learning.

Students, faculty, and staff must develop skills in the use and application of technology.

Environmental awareness and responsibility are critical. For this reason, the school is a focal point for the ISKL community.

Figure 6.4. Statement of school district core values and beliefs: A sample.

COUNSELING PROGRAM CORE BELIEFS
OF SCHOOL DISTRICT B

1. Each student is affected by physical, social, emotional, intellectual, environmental, and behavioral factors. These factors are constantly at play within the milieu of the school and community. This milieu is created by the people who play, work, engage in social activities with each other, and participate as parents, children, and relatives within families. The community's quality of life is affected by the nature and effectiveness of families, schools, recreation programs, health services, religions, and other social institutions available to each individual throughout his or her life.

2. Human life seeks to enhance its own existence. Therefore, each student is motivated by positive growth forces that push toward the enhancement of life and learning. At this most fundamental level, all children and adolescents are viewed as positively motivated toward attaining the best growth, learning, and achievement possible. Within the parameters established by the social milieu of the school and community, each young person must find the nurturance to grow, the opportunities to learn, the values to live by, and adult models to follow.

3. Students are fundamentally social. Therefore, they must develop basic social skills that are acceptable within their own families and community. This process of learning provides ample opportunity for each student to feel valued, to feel important, and to belong. All students must have opportunities to develop skills in understanding themselves and others as well as formal assistance in developing effective interpersonal communication skills—skills that form the basis for accurate and appropriate social involvement and healthy disclosure of self in intimate relationships.

4. Students respond best when expectations are defined and communicated in an atmosphere of mutual respect and openness. Therefore, the assumption is that all staff members have the

same needs and also function best in a similar atmosphere, which offers the same opportunities to adults as is offered to the youth within the school.

Figure 6.5. Counseling program core beliefs presented as statements: A sample.

In Figure 6.6, you see an example of how the statements from Figure 6.5 could be abbreviated.

Figures 6.3 and 6.5 illustrate statements that emphasize sociological and psychological aspects of student development. A program of services based on this emphasis is likely to stress psychosocial development and encourage planning around psychosocial needs. Again, the way that beliefs and values are formulated and the content of those statements sets the tone for further planning.

COUNSELING PROGRAM CORE BELIEFS OF SCHOOL DISTRICT B, ABBREVIATED FORM

We Believe:

Each student is influenced by the home, school, and community.

Each student seeks to enhance his or her own life and learning.

Social learning is essential to student growth and development.

Growth and development occur best in an atmosphere of mutual respect and openness.

Figure 6.6. Counseling program core beliefs stated in abbreviated form: A sample.

Core beliefs and governing values convey a sense of what is important to each district and form the foundation for each district's curricular emphasis, as well as the focus of its student services. Reaching consensus on core governing values and beliefs leads to clear statements of those beliefs and values, which in turn permits the district planning to proceed in a congruent and coherent manner.

Similarly, the core beliefs held by counselors serve as the foundation upon which effective and purposeful planning can be built. A consensus foundation of beliefs and values is the beginning of a coherent support system from which a program of strength and integrity can be constructed. Reaching a consensus through exploring and clarifying beliefs and values will sustain the planning effort and add strength to the completed plan.

THE VISION STATEMENT

A vision statement is a description of the ideals that inspire and motivate participants toward the future. It lays out, in one or two paragraphs, the ideal standards of excellence and the ideal, fully developed, implemented, and evaluated school counseling program. Generally, the entire counseling staff should participate in creating the vision statement. You should idealize, visualize, and imagine a perfected state of expert functioning for the entire counseling and guidance program. Arriving at a vision statement can be an inspiring and motivational exercise for counselors and can enhance understanding and cohesiveness. The counseling coordinator, an administrator, or a designated team leader can help in creating a vision statement. The leader can use any number of activities and exercises. The following are examples of how counselors in a district can create a vision statement.

Collecting Our Visions

Groups of 15 or fewer can complete this process in less than 45 minutes. In groups of fewer than 5, each person should go through all the steps and share his or her experience with the group.

Step 1. Have participants take a few minutes to relax, close their eyes, and imagine what it might be like five or six years from now to work as a counselor in the "best of all worlds counseling program."

Step 2. After a few minutes ask participants to imagine the kinds of things they would be doing, how they would feel, what they would see around them, how teachers and administrators would behave, and what students would say.

Step 3. In a few more minutes, have participants form dyads and ask each person to share as much detail as he or she wants with his or her partner.

Step 4. When the pairs have finished sharing their visions of the future, ask each to report to the larger group. Ask for any common themes, content, or experiences. Write items from each pair on a chalkboard, overhead, or paper visible to the entire group.

Step 5. Lead an open, large-group discussion about the common themes, differences, and unique contributions of the various items listed.

Step 6. Form small groups (with no more than five in each) to draft a vision statement drawn from all the vision items generated.

Step 7. Have each group share by writing on the board the vision statement it prepared.

Step 8. Ask each group to revise its vision statement after reading all vision statements from all groups and after the large-group discussion.

Step 9. Share revised vision statements again and discuss the final vision statement. Have the entire group decide how to prepare a final statement for acceptance by the counseling staff.

Paradise Imagined

A Writing Exercise. Have each participant write a one-page description of the counseling and guidance program in an imagined paradise. Create a vivid description of the success attained as a counselor in paradise within the next five years. Describe specifics of the people, physical environment, the experiences during one day, or in any other ways describe the state of affairs in paradise. Encourage creativity and dreaming.

A Group Discussion.

Step 1. Organize small groups to brainstorm *Paradise Imagined* with descriptive notes. Allow 10 to 12 minutes for this.

Step 2. Have each group report in detail to the larger group.

Step 3. List key items from each group description in a format visible to the entire group.

Step 4. Discuss and clarify.

Step 5. Select a writing group to draft a vision statement for further consideration.

These activities should produce a vision statement for the school counseling program (see Figure 6.7). Professional leaders of the counseling and guidance team provide power through the vision. A shared vision among all counselors in a district will invigorate teachers, administrators, and community helpers.

SCHOOL COUNSELING PROGRAM
VISION STATEMENT

Remember, vision is the idealized heart, feeling, and caring message of the counseling and guidance program.

Figure 6.7. School counseling program vision statement: A sample.

MISSION STATEMENT

The mission statement brings direction and focus and expresses the commitment of the counseling program. It establishes a marker for making all decisions about how resources—including time, money, and expertise—will be allocated. The mission statement also may set criteria against which any agenda can be measured.

The mission statement communicates to the public the purposes and promises behind the delivery of counseling and guidance services. It puts together, in a few words, a clear message about purpose, uniqueness, commitment, and values, and brings into one short, concise statement the unique and unifying directions of the program. The example in Figure 6.8, from the counselors at the American School in Japan, shows how the special circumstances in an international school bring focus to the work of the school's counselors.

In contrast to the vision statement, a mission statement should be developed with input from all stakeholders. These stakeholders are represented by members of the advisory team. The mission statement is the first group task of the advisory team. Once the vision statement has been reviewed and understood by the advisory team, work may proceed on the mission statement.

MISSION STATEMENT FROM THE COUNSELING PROGRAM AT THE AMERICAN SCHOOL IN JAPAN

The mission of the guidance and counseling program is to promote emotional health, interpersonal skills, physical development and academic success in an international setting where cultural sensitivity, transition issues, and family support are special concerns.

Figure 6.8. School counseling program mission statement: A sample.

Different groups use different approaches to develop a mission statement. Having all members of the advisory team involved is essential, because the mission statement provides direction and meaning that is communicated to the school and the community.

Once consensus is reached on core values, vision, and mission, the foundation for a comprehensive counseling and guidance program is in place. This foundation provides the philosophical and conceptual basis for designing structure in program planning.

Chapter 7

NEEDS ASSESSMENTS, GOALS, AND OBJECTIVES

The framework of the counseling and guidance program rests on the foundations of core values, vision, and mission. Framing the program begins with determining the needs of the various stakeholders and setting program goals. After your goals are in place, you should set objectives to ensure that the program continues to serve the mission. This chapter sets forth a process for assessing needs, setting goals, and writing objectives, with specific samples of each.

NEEDS ASSESSMENT IN THE SCHOOL COMMUNITY

You should conduct needs assessment once you have attained consensus on the core beliefs, vision, and mission of the counseling program. Assessing needs gives you information that will help you make choices about priorities and goals. Having data that document needs provides evidence and focus for spending time, expertise, and other resources. Assessing needs is the first step in answering the question, "What is to be done?"

There are several ways to conduct needs assessments. Some common approaches include paper/pencil surveys, structured interviews, and focus groups. An advisory team decision on the most appropriate option should consider the time, expertise, and monetary resources available. We recommend that the advisory team assess counseling-related needs within the following groups: students, parents, teachers, administrators, employers, and business and government leaders.

Your advisory team will want to review various formats for conducting needs assessment. You should use methods that give quantitative evidence of needs rather than those that rely primarily on subjective perceptions. You also should pay careful attention to a procedure's comprehensiveness. Remember, however, that you should not assess needs in areas for which services will not be available. Your efforts, energy, and time are best devoted to assessing needs in those areas for which you will provide services. A comprehensive needs assessment procedure includes items related to the personal, social, educational, and career areas of concern to students, parents, and school staff.

Paper-and-pencil surveys usually are efficient for obtaining the largest sampling and building a database of information. The particular items to be used usually are chosen in the first planning year. The advisory team should develop appropriate methods for publicity, distribution, return, and tabulation of the surveys.

Format

At the end of this chapter, you will find several sample needs assessment instruments. Figures 7.1 through 7.12 are paper-and-pencil type surveys, and Figure 7.13 is an interview instrument. Keep in mind that these surveys were constructed to address needs specific to each school and community. Simply extracting the examples may be expedient, but the items and formats presented may not adequately define the particular needs of your school. We offer these examples simply as models; you should adapt the individual items to your school's needs. When distributing the surveys, we recommend including a cover letter that explains its purpose and detailed instructions for returning the completed survey to the school. As you look over the examples, you will note that items are parallel across populations and that each survey is written at the reading level of the target age group: Figures 7.1 through 7.3 are written for the senior high level; Figures 7.4 through 7.6 are aimed at junior high; and Figures 7.7 through 7.11 are appropriate for upper and lower elementary school students.

Parallel Construction

Parallel construction of items across all grade levels and populations offers certain advantages:

1. The surveys are easily administered to students by classroom teachers in a short time.

2. All populations can express their needs honestly.

3. Parent and teacher/administrator surveys correspond to student surveys, at all grade levels.

4. They provide for congruence across populations in the ranking of needs.

5. The scoring is neither complicated nor time-consuming.

Scoring

Surveys are scored by adding the numbers circled for each statement from all surveys. Statements receiving the highest total numbers are the top-priority needs. The kindergarten through third-grade surveys are scored by tabulating the number of responses marked "yes" and the number marked "no." Statements marked "yes" most frequently are the highest-priority needs. In other words, the items marked "yes" most often get the highest priority ranking.[1]

[1] Items for the sample needs assessment surveys in Figures 7.1 through 7.12 were adapted from Hamilton and Henley (1988). Needs assessment item bank: Appendix C. In The Kansas Guidance Program Evaluation Guide Resource Packet.

NEEDS ASSESSMENT IN THE LARGER COMMUNITY

Surveys

It sometimes is helpful to survey community business owners and managers. Needs statements for this group should be written following the same format as that used in the teacher/administrator surveys. In addition, you can include statements that address student needs related to job training (e.g., "Students need to learn about the importance of personal appearance in seeking and keeping jobs" and "Counselors need to consult with employers concerning student employment"). In Figure 7.12 you will find a sample that could be used with businesses in your community.

The needs assessment may include the total population in your community or a smaller representative sample from each group. Surveying a selected percentage of students and parents and all teachers and administrators is one approach. The size of the school district and the resources available often dictates how extensive your survey can be. Choosing a random sample from each group reduces the number of instruments required as well as the time needed for administration and tabulation. Random samples of 10% to 25% of the total population generally is adequate when the size of a community makes a survey of the total population impractical. Parent surveys can be mailed; be sure to include stamped, preaddressed envelopes for returning the surveys. All student surveys can be completed in class and collected by teachers.

Interviews

Another way to conduct needs assessment is by personal or telephone interviews. If your advisory team chooses this method, you must make certain that a random sample of the population of each stakeholder group is interviewed. The percentage is left to the discretion of counselors and the advisory team. A carefully selected random sample of 1,200 persons is sufficient for national polls and is accurate to within 2 to 3 percentage points. Many factors must be considered when conducting such a poll, and expertise in sampling might be needed in defining the relevant variables. In smaller districts, a larger percentage of the population can be interviewed if sufficient help is available.

One advantage of the interview method is that it provides for direct contact with populations served by the counseling program. A sample interview format is shown in Figure 7.13. It does not take much time to complete, and the respondent has an opportunity to voice any additional concerns or to ask questions. Such comments may be helpful in determining definite strengths and weaknesses as well as providing suggestions and constructive criticisms. Generally, much less effort is required to analyze the results of telephone interviews. The major disadvantages include the number of people it takes to phone or visit each respondent and possible difficulties in contacting parents.

Focus Groups

Another approach to needs assessment is to conduct focus groups. One advantage of this approach is the opportunity it provides for discussion and clarification of various points of view regarding counseling and guidance needs. To obtain data on needs from focus groups, you should develop a series of open-ended questions to stimulate discussion among group members. The group leader should plan to guide discussion toward the predetermined topics and set a tone that encourages expression of diverse views.

You should select members for focus groups from each stakeholder group. High school and adult groups may be as large as 12 to 18 persons. Student groups should be from homogeneous developmental levels. Each group of parents, students, teachers, community leaders, or employers will state opinions from their own perspective and thereby add to the data pool. In addition to a leader, it is helpful to have an observer in your focus group who takes notes, tracks opinions, and monitors levels of intensity.

The needs assessment samples presented here can help you think about the kinds of items you want to include when conducting your own needs assessment. A well-conducted paper/pencil survey, interview, or focus group discussion can help your advisory team decide on the focus of your program.

EVALUATING THE RESULTS

The advisory team should analyze and evaluate the needs assessment data to determine the highest-priority needs and to set program goals. Using student workers from the counseling center, office/business classes, or data entry classes can speed up the process of compiling results. Once the data have been compiled, the next step is to rank each need within each population, then study the ranked needs and prioritize them for each population group. This process can be completed for each building or for each grade level in larger school systems.

The advisory team should study the rankings of each representative group and then decide how much weight to give those rankings within each stakeholder group. Results from students often differ from those obtained from parents and teachers. The advisory team may decide to give student rankings a higher weighting when determining the overall priority rankings. The team also may decide to investigate further (i.e., by conducting interviews with students) when wide differences occur between stakeholder groups in priority rankings. Interpreting the differences in priority rankings is essential before you can move on to setting goals.

Figures 7.14 through 7.19 show samples of rankings drawn from the tabulation of results from actual needs assessment surveys. By comparing results from different school levels—Figures 7.14 and 7.15 are from senior highs; Figures 7.16 and 7.17 from junior highs; and Figures 7.18 and 7.19 from elementary schools— we get an idea of how results can vary among stakeholder groups and grade levels. Figures 7.15, 7.17, and 7.19 show how the advisory team placed needs into a ranking for different levels within a school system.

The first year of advisory team planning should be devoted to completing assessing needs, establishing priorities, and developing goals for the very highest priorities. Most schools will want to begin planning implementation for only the top three to five priority needs during the first year. Implementation based on the top three to five priorities should be initiated and continued for at least one year before additional priority needs are addressed. The advisory team, counseling staff, and administrative staff should keep in mind that an excellent counseling program evolves only over a period of five or six years.

MAKING THE PLAN WORK

The counseling program must be planned, implemented, monitored, and evaluated in a systematic way. Goals should be established only after needs have been identified and prioritized. Once the goals have been set, objectives should be developed to mark the path toward the goals.

Goals

Deciding on goals for a program requires study of the prioritized needs. The advisory team should decide on only a small number of goals for the first year of implementation. Each goal should be written to reflect the identified and prioritized needs within each domain. Before goal statements are adopted, each member of the counseling staff and the advisory team should consider the resources available and any other factors that may affect the attainment of each goal.

Goal statements mark the destinations agreed upon by all parties. There are two basic types of goals:

1. those that set the targets in program management or process, and

2. those that specify the outcomes or results intended for the various program activities.

Program Management Goals. Management goals show the agenda of planned activities. Having a set of program management goals lets you know in advance what major activities will be occurring at what time and who will be responsible for them. Having a clear set of program management goals also allows you to publicly schedule activities for any specified time frame. A year-long calendar can be posted and distributed. Some counselors use magic markers to color code by day or week the major events planned for the month or year.

Examples of Management Goals

• To identify, appoint, and train an advisory team

• To conduct a community-wide needs assessment

Program Outcome Goals. Program outcome goals specify the desired results of program functions. They identify the final outcome of the counselors' efforts. Selecting and writing goals is a vital part of deciding what is expected in the way of achievements or accomplishments in regard to the identified needs. Each program goal statement specifies a desired outcome for students, school staff, parents, or others.

Examples of Program Goals

• To improve career decision-making skills of high school students

• To increase students' positive perception of themselves

Goal statements identify the final destination following participation in a series of counseling activities.

Objectives

In contrast to goals, objectives specify points of progress along a path toward a goal. They ensure measurability and show precisely what is to be achieved at each step in the process. Objectives are also of two types:

1. management or process objectives and

2. program outcome objectives.

Management/Process Objectives. Management or process objectives are those which specify the points of progress along the paths established by the management goals. Usually several objectives are required for each goal, because moving toward the goal almost always requires many separate steps.

Examples of Management/Process Objectives

Management goal: To identify, appoint, and train an advisory team

> *Management objective 1.* By the end of October, counselors will have completed selection and appointment of the advisory team as evidenced by signed acceptance notices on file with a scheduled orientation meeting of the advisory team.

> *Management objective 2.* By the end of December, orientation, organization, and training of the advisory team will be completed as evidenced by completed evaluation forms from the training workshop

Program Outcome Objectives. Program outcome objectives show specifically how, when, under what conditions, and to what levels of performance a specified outcome will be attained. For objectives to be usable in meeting the specified goal, they must

- be related to the goal,

- be realistic and obtainable,

- identify specific actions, and

- include criteria for determining that the outcome has been attained.

Just as with management objectives, in order to meet the stated goal it usually is necessary to include several outcome objectives.

Examples of Program Outcome Objectives

Program goal: To improve career decision-making skills of high school students

Program objective 1. After participating in a series of classroom group activities designed to help them identify and understand their own interests, 90% of students participating will be able to write four special interests and list those occupations most closely related to those interests.

Program objective 2. After completing 10 one-hour counselor-led group sessions on decision making and planning, group members will be able to complete a detailed personal plan showing their progress toward specific career goals.

Developing goals and objectives that specifically address prioritized needs brings specificity and order to the counseling program. Developing clear and relevant goals and objectives is among the most difficult tasks for most teams. Failing to write objectives in measurable outcomes and writing too many detailed objectives or too few are common errors.

Gathering good data leads to consensus on priorities and clear goals; this sets the stage for selecting appropriate strategies. One other critical step is to *take an honest inventory of available resources before adopting goals and objectives*. Little will be accomplished other than frustration and disappointment if adequate resources are not available to conduct the program.

DECIDING ON ACTIVITIES

Once the advisory team has decided on goals and objectives, it is time to plan the activities and strategies for the preventive and educational components of the program. It is impossible for counselors and teachers to develop on their own all or even most of the specific programs needed to accomplish all of the goals. Therefore, we suggest you consider commercially developed activities. You can and should adapt any of these programs to your specific needs. Simply adopting a program in totality for convenience's sake may undercut or delay achievement of your program's goals. Pick and choose those activities that address specific objectives.

For example, you may choose activities from several different sources and integrate them into a unique plan.

A Preventive Resource Activity Guide

You may want to write a counseling and guidance program activity guide outlining activity plans addressing each objective. Each activity plan should include instructions for conducting the activity, copies of student activity sheets, and pre- and post-assessment instruments. The activity guide should be divided into four sections:

1. Personal, behavioral, and emotional skills needs

2. Social actions and skills needs

3. Educational performance and future planning needs

4. Lifestyle and career future needs

Each school level should have its own activity guide.

When developing a set of activities, you should consider several factors, including these:

1. The activities must relate to top-priority needs as determined by the needs assessment and the advisory team.

2. The activities must be suitable for the age or grade range for which they are proposed.

3. There must be a balance between affective and cognitive activities.

4. Each activity relates directly to at least one program outcome objective.

5. Materials are available for conducting the activity.

6. Properly trained counselors and teachers are available to conduct or supervise the activities.

If these factors are not considered, the probability of accomplishing the objectives is extremely low. Chapter 9 presents examples of how materials and strategies are coordinated for meeting identified priority needs.

Figure 7.20 shows samples of goals, objectives, and activities that address the priority needs for an elementary school—as identified through the ranking process described earlier in the chapter. Note that the sample strategies and activities are listed after the objectives.

Figure 7.1. Needs assessment survey for senior high school students. A sample.

Mill Creek Senior High School

Counseling Program Needs Assessment Survey
Grades 10, 11, and 12
Student Survey

The counseling and administrative staff and the Counseling Program Advisory Team of the Mill Creek School District need your help in identifying the needs of students, parents, school personnel, and the community which can be served by school counselors and the counseling program. The following survey will be of great value in helping us identify needs as well as indicating those areas with which you are satisfied.

Instructions: Please respond to all information on the top of the survey instrument and then follow the directions directly above the survey. When you have completed, your teacher will collect the surveys and return them to the counseling center.

Figure 7.1. Continued.

Mill Creek Senior High School Needs Survey
Student Version

Circle your grade level:　　10　　11　　12

Instructions: Circle the number you think most closely or best reflects the level of need you have for each of the items in the statements below.

Personal Behavioral and Emotional Skills

	high	low

1. I need to learn to experience self-awareness and self-acceptance.　　　　　　　4 3 2 1

2. I need to understand myself and my actions.　　　　　　4 3 2 1

3. I need to be aware of my strengths and weaknesses.　　　　4 3 2 1

4. I need to be more honest with others about how I really feel.　　　　　　　4 3 2 1

5. I need to learn to deal with my feelings in effective ways.　　　　　　　4 3 2 1

6. I need to learn to deal with death and dying.　　　　4 3 2 1

7. I need to learn to deal with parental divorce.　　　　4 3 2 1

8. I need to be educated about drugs and alcohol and their effects on my life.　　　　　　　4 3 2 1

Social Actions and Skills

9. I need to learn to share my needs, ideas, and feelings with others.　　　　　　　4 3 2 1

10. I need to learn to stand up for myself in a group.　　　4 3 2 1

11. I need to learn to be more tolerant of people whose views, appearance, or actions differ from my own.　　4 3 2 1

12. I need to learn about love, marriage, and family living.　4 3 2 1

13. I need to learn how to get along better with members of my family.　　　　　　　4 3 2 1

14. I need to learn how to help my parents accept my friends.　　　　　　　4 3 2 1

Figure 7.1. Continued.

15. I need to become more aware of my responsibilities at home.   4 3 2 1

16. I need to learn to work with counselors and administrators.   4 3 2 1

Educational Performance and Future Planning

17. I need to become aware of available counseling services.   4 3 2 1

18. I need information about graduation requirements.   4 3 2 1

19. I need to improve my study skills and habits.   4 3 2 1

20. I need to develop test-taking skills.   4 3 2 1

21. I need to improve my ability to concentrate.   4 3 2 1

22. I need help in understanding my test scores   .4 3 2 1

23. I need to learn how to apply school learning to the non-school environment.   4 3 2 1

24. I need information about educational alternatives after high school.   4 3 2 1

Lifestyle and Career Future

25. I need to explore my interests, abilities, and aptitudes.   4 3 2 1

26. I need information about training, skills required, and the future of certain occupations.   4 3 2 1

27. I need information about the job market.   4 3 2 1

28. I need to know how to pursue a definite career plan.   4 3 2 1

29. I need help in selecting my career goals.   4 3 2 1

30. I need to learn how to identify the requirements for my career choices.   4 3 2 1

31. I need the opportunity for on-the-job experience in my career interest area.   4 3 2 1

32. I need to understand the effect work has on my life.   4 3 2 1

Figure 7.2. Needs assessment survey for parents of senior high school students: A sample.

Mill Creek Senior High School

Counseling Program Needs Assessment Survey
Grades 10, 11, and 12
Parent Survey

The counseling and administrative staff and the counseling program advisor team of the Mill Creek School District need your help in identifying the needs of students, parents, school personnel, and the community which can be served by the school counselors and the counseling program. The following survey will be of great value in helping us identify needs as well as indicating those areas with which you are satisfied.

If you have any questions, call the counseling center (Tel 555-0000). You may mail your completed survey to the school, deliver it if you plan to be visiting the school, or send it with your son or daughter. Please return your completed survey within five days. Thank you for your time and interest.

Figure 7.2. Continued.

Mill Creek Senior High School Needs Survey
Parent Version

Circle the grade level of your son or daughter: **10 11 12**

Instructions: Circle the number which you think most closely or best reflects the level of need your child or you have for each of the items in the statements below.

	high			low

1. My child needs to learn to experience self-awareness and self-acceptance.   4 3 2 1

2. My child needs to understand him- or herself and his or her actions.   4 3 2 1

3. My child needs to be aware of his or her strengths and weaknesses.   4 3 2 1

4. My child needs to be more honest with others about how he or she really feels.   4 3 2 1

5. My child needs to learn to deal with his or her feelings in effective ways.   4 3 2 1

6. My child needs to learn to deal with death and dying.   4 3 2 1

7. My child needs to learn to deal with parental divorce.   4 3 2 1

8. My child needs to be educated about drugs and alcohol and their effects on life.   4 3 2 1

9. My child needs to learn to share his or her needs, ideas, and feelings with others.   4 3 2 1

10. My child needs to learn to stand up for him- or herself in a group.   4 3 2 1

11. My child needs to learn to be more tolerant of people whose views, appearance, or actions differ from his or her own   4 3 2 1

12. My child needs to learn about love, marriage, and family living.   4 3 2 1

13. My child needs to learn how to get along better with members of his or her family.   4 3 2 1

Figure 7.2. Continued.

14. My child needs to learn how to help us to accept his
or her friends. 4 3 2 1

15. My child needs to become more aware of his or her
responsibilities at home. 4 3 2 1

16. My child needs to learn to work with the counselor
and administrators. 4 3 2 1

17. My child needs to become aware of available
counseling services. 4 3 2 1

18. My child needs information about graduation
requirements. 4 3 2 1

19. My child needs to improve his or her study skills
and habits. 4 3 2 1

20. My child needs to develop test-taking skills. 4 3 2 1

21. My child needs to improve his or her ability to
concentrate. 4 3 2 1

22. My child needs help in understanding his or her
standardized test scores. 4 3 2 1

23. My child needs to learn how to apply school learning
to the non-school environment. 4 3 2 1

24. My child needs information about educational
alternatives after high school. 4 3 2 1

25. My child needs to explore his or her interests, abilities,
and aptitudes. 4 3 2 1

26. My child needs information about training, skills
required, and the future of certain occupations. 4 3 2 1

27. My child needs information about the job market. 4 3 2 1

28. My child needs to know how to pursue a definite
career plan. 4 3 2 1

29. My child needs help in selecting his or her career goals. 4 3 2 1

30. My child needs to learn how to identify the
requirements for his or her career choices. 4 3 2 1

Figure 7.2. Continued.

31. My child needs the opportunity for on-the-job
experience in his or her career interest area.   4 3 2 1

32. My child needs to understand the effect work has on
his or her life.   4 3 2 1

33. I need to know what my child's standardized test
scores mean.   4 3 2 1

34. I need to know more about the counseling program and
what services the counselor can provide me as a parent. 4 3 2 1

35. I need more information regarding educational
opportunities for my child.   4 3 2 1

36. I need to learn more effective parenting skills.   4 3 2 1

37. I need to see the counselor concerning my child's needs. 4 3 2 1

38. I need to develop a better relationship with my child's
teachers.   4 3 2 1

39. I need information on how to apply for financial aid
for my child's college education.   4 3 2 1

40. I need information about job opportunities for my child. 4 3 2 1

Figure 7.3. Needs assessment survey for teachers and administrators in a senior high school: A sample.

Mill Creek Senior High School

Counseling Program Needs Assessment Survey
Grades 10, 11, and 12
Teacher and Administrator Survey

The Counseling Program Advisory Team for our school district needs your help in identifying the needs of students, parents, school personnel, and the community which can be served by the school counselors and the counseling program. The following survey will be of great value in helping us identify needs as well as indicating those areas with which you are satisfied.

If you have any questions, please see any member of the counseling staff or contact a member of the Counseling Program Advisory Team. When you have completed the survey, return it to the counseling center. Please return your completed survey within five days. Thank you for your time and interest.

Figure 7.3. Continued.

Mill Creek Senior High School Needs Survey
Teachers and Administrators Version

Circle the grade level(s) you teach or supervise: **10 11 12**

Instructions: Circle the number which you think most closely or best represents the level of need for each of the following:

	high			low

1. Students need to learn to experience self-awareness and self-acceptance.   4 3 2 1

2. Students need to understand themselves and their actions.   4 3 2 1

3. Students need to be aware of their strengths and weaknesses.   4 3 2 1

4. Students need to be more honest with others about how they really feel.   4 3 2 1

5. Students need to learn to deal with their feelings in effective ways.   4 3 2 1

6. Students need to learn to deal with death and dying.   4 3 2 1

7. Students need to learn to deal with parental divorce.   4 3 2 1

8. Students need to be educated about drugs and alcohol and their effects on life.   4 3 2 1

9. Students need to learn to share their needs, ideas, and feelings with others.   4 3 2 1

10. Students need to learn to stand up for themselves in a group.   4 3 2 1

11. Students need to learn to be more tolerant of people whose views, appearance, or actions differ from their own.   4 3 2 1

12. Students need to learn about love, marriage, and family living.   4 3 2 1

13. Students need to learn how to get along better with members of their families.   4 3 2 1

14. Students need to learn how to help their parents accept their friends.   4 3 2 1

Figure 7.3. Continued.

15. Students need to become more aware of their
responsibilities at home.   4 3 2 1

16. Students need to learn to work with the counselors
and administrators.   4 3 2 1

17. Students need to become aware of available
counseling services.   4 3 2 1

18. Students need information on graduation requirements. 4 3 2 1

19. Students need to improve their study skills and habits. 4 3 2 1

20. Students need to develop test-taking skills. 4 3 2 1

21. Students need to improve their ability to concentrate. 4 3 2 1

22. Students need help in understanding their standardized
test scores.   4 3 2 1

23. Students need to learn how to apply school learning
to the non-school environment.   4 3 2 1

24. Students need information about educational
alternatives after high school.   4 3 2 1

25. Students need to explore their interests, abilities, and
aptitudes.   4 3 2 1

26. Students need information about training, skills
required, and the future of certain occupations. 4 3 2 1

27. Students need information about the job market. 4 3 2 1

28. Students need to know how to pursue career plans. 4 3 2 1

29. Students need help in selecting their career goals. 4 3 2 1

30. Students need to learn how to identify the requirements
for their career choices.   4 3 2 1

31. Students need the opportunity for on-the-job experience
in their career interest area.   4 3 2 1

32. Students need to understand the effect work has on life. 4 3 2 1

33. I need to know more about reviewing and interpreting
student records.   4 3 2 1

Figure 7.3. Continued.

34. I need to know more about referring students to
the counselor.   4 3 2 1

35. I need to know more about making student referrals
for special education classes.   4 3 2 1

36. I need to know more about curriculum development
and how to be more involved in this process.   4 3 2 1

37. I need to know how to meet the needs of all my students. 4 3 2 1

38. I need to know how to communicate more openly with
students.   4 3 2 1

39. I need help communicating with parents more
effectively.   4 3 2 1

40. I need to develop a better relationship with the
counselor.   4 3 2 1

41. I need more information on college and vocational
opportunities for my students.   4 3 2 1

42. I think the school needs to provide more opportunities
for staff development via in-service workshops.   4 3 2 1

Figure 7.4. Needs assessment survey for junior high school students: A sample.

Cherokee Falls Junior High School

Counseling Program Needs Assessment Survey
Grades 7, 8, and 9
Student Survey

The counseling staff and the Counseling Program Advisory Team for the Mill Creek School District need your help in identifying the needs of students in our school. Your responses on this survey will be of great value in helping develop a counseling program that can more effectively meet your needs.

Instructions: Circle your grade level. After reading each statement, circle the number that corresponds most closely to your need. Respond to each statement honestly—no one will have access to your responses. When everyone has completed the survey, your teacher will collect the surveys and send them to the counseling center.

Figure 7.4. Continued.

Cherokee Falls Junior High School Needs Survey
Student Version

Circle your grade level: 7 8 9

Instructions: Circle the number you feel best fits the level of need for each of the following statements.

	high			low

1. I need to understand how my feelings affect my behavior. 4 3 2 1

2. I need to learn how to express my feelings more easily. 4 3 2 1

3. I need to understand death. 4 3 2 1

4. I need to understand separation and divorce. 4 3 2 1

5. I need to better understand the effects of alcohol and drugs. 4 3 2 1

6. I need to be responsible for my actions. 4 3 2 1

7. I need to stand up for myself in a group instead of being a follower all the time. 4 3 2 1

8. I need to be more tolerant of people whose views differ from mine. 4 3 2 1

9. I need to know how to get along better with members of the opposite sex. 4 3 2 1

10. I need help in better understanding adults. 4 3 2 1

11. I need to understand better what my parents expect of me. 4 3 2 1

12. I need to talk more with the counselor. 4 3 2 1

13. I need to be better informed about the services available through the counseling program. 4 3 2 1

14. I need to improve my study skills. 4 3 2 1

15. I need to learn how the things I study in school will be useful outside of school. 4 3 2 1

16. I need to know which courses are required and which are electives. 4 3 2 1

Figure 7.4. Continued.

17. I need to learn how to take tests.   4   3   2   1

18. I need to know more about my ability to do school work.   4   3   2   1

19. I need to know more about what workers must learn
to do for jobs I might like.   4   3   2   1

20. I need to make plans for developing abilities needed
in my career interest areas.   4   3   2   1

21. I need to understand more about the effect work will
have on my life.   4   3   2   1

22. I need to know how to find out what jobs are available
to me locally.   4   3   2   1

23. I need to know how to apply for a job.   4   3   2   1

24. I need to know what to do and say in a job interview.   4   3   2   1

Figure 7.5. Needs assessment survey for parents of junior high school students: A sample.

Cherokee Falls Junior High School

Counseling Program Needs Assessment Survey
Grades 7, 8, and 9
Parent Survey

The counseling staff and the Counseling Program Advisory Team for the Mill Creek School District request your assistance in identifying the needs of students, parents, teachers/administrators, and the community in our school district. With your help, the counseling staff can serve identified priority needs more effectively.

Instructions: After completing the requested information at the top of the survey, read each statement carefully and then circle the number you believe most closely corresponds to the need. When you have completed the survey, return it to the counseling center. You may deliver it personally, mail it, or send it to school with your son or daughter. Please respond to this survey within a week. Thank you for your interest and assistance.

Figure 7.5. Continued.

Cherokee Falls Junior High School Needs Survey
Parent Version

Circle the grade level of your child: 7   8   9

Instructions: Circle the number you feel best fits the level of need for each of the following statements.

		high			low
1.	My child needs to learn how feelings affect his or her behavior.	4	3	2	1
2.	My child needs to learn to express his or her feelings more easily.	4	3	2	1
3.	My child needs to learn how to deal with death and dying.	4	3	2	1
4.	My child needs to learn how to deal with divorce.	4	3	2	1
5.	My child needs to be educated about drugs and alcohol and their effects.	4	3	2	1
6.	My child needs to develop a sense of responsibility.	4	3	2	1
7.	My child needs to become aware of personal expectations and attitudes in social situations.	4	3	2	1
8.	My child needs to learn to be more tolerant and accepting of people who are different.	4	3	2	1
9.	My child needs to learn how to be friends with members of the opposite sex.	4	3	2	1
10.	My child needs to learn to better communicate with adults.	4	3	2	1
11.	My child needs to be more aware of parental expectations.	4	3	2	1
12.	My child needs to talk to the counselor.	4	3	2	1
13.	My child needs to learn more about available counseling services.	4	3	2	1
14.	My child needs to improve his or her study habits.	4	3	2	1
15.	My child needs to learn how school learning applies to the non-school environment.	4	3	2	1

Figure 7.5. Continued.

16. My child needs information about required and elective
    courses.   4 3 2 1

17. My child needs to learn how to take tests.   4 3 2 1

18. My child needs to know what his or her academic
    abilities are.   4 3 2 1

19. My child needs to learn requirements for career
    choices and to select career goals.   4 3 2 1

20. My child needs to understand his or her interests,
    abilities, and aptitudes.   4 3 2 1

21. My child needs to understand the effect work has on
    one's life.   4 3 2 1

22. My child needs information about jobs in the
    community.   4 3 2 1

23. My child needs to know how to apply for a job.   4 3 2 1

24. My child needs to know what to say and do during
    a job interview.   4 3 2 1

25. I need to know more about the counseling program.   4 3 2 1

26. I need more information regarding educational
    opportunities for my child.   4 3 2 1

27. I need information about the special education program. 4 3 2 1

28. I need to learn more effective parenting skills.   4 3 2 1

29. I need to visit with the counselor concerning my
    child's needs.   4 3 2 1

30. I need to develop a better relationship with my
    child's teachers.   4 3 2 1

Figure 7.6. Needs assessment survey for teachers and administrators in a junior high school: A sample.

Cherokee Falls Junior High School

Counseling Program Needs Assessment Survey
Grades 7, 8, and 9
Teacher and Administrator Survey

The counseling staff and the Counseling Program Advisory Team for the Mill Creek School District request your assistance in identifying the needs of students, parents, teachers/administrators, and the community. With your help, the counseling staff can serve identified priority needs more effectively.

Instructions: After completing the requested information at the top of the survey, read each statement carefully and then circle the number you believe most closely corresponds to the need. When you have completed the survey, return it to the counseling center. Please respond to this survey within a week. Thank you for your interest and assistance.

Figure 7.6. Continued.

Cherokee Falls Junior High School Needs Survey
Teacher and Administrator Version

Circle the grade level(s) you teach or supervise: 7   8   9

Instructions: Circle the number you feel best fits the level of need for each of the following statements.

		high			low
1.	Students need to understand themselves and their actions.	4	3	2	1
2.	Students need help in gaining awareness of their feelings about themselves.	4	3	2	1
3.	Students need to know how to deal with death and dying.	4	3	2	1
4.	Students need to learn how to deal with parental divorce.	4	3	2	1
5.	Students need to know about the dangers of drugs and alcohol.	4	3	2	1
6.	Students need to learn to take responsibility for their actions.	4	3	2	1
7.	Students need to learn to make their own decisions rather than follow the group.	4	3	2	1
8.	Students need to be more tolerant of people whose views, appearances, or actions differ from their own.	4	3	2	1
9.	Students need to learn how to establish friendships with members of the opposite sex.	4	3	2	1
10.	Students need to learn to communicate more effectively with adults.	4	3	2	1
11.	Students need to be aware of parental expectations.	4	3	2	1
12.	Students need to spend more time with the counselor.	4	3	2	1
13.	Students need to learn more about services offered by the counselor.	4	3	2	1
14.	Students need help in learning study skills.	4	3	2	1
15.	Students need to learn more about the importance of success in school.	4	3	2	1

Figure 7.6. Continued.

16. Students need to learn more about course requirements. 4 3 2 1

17. Students need to learn how to take tests. 4 3 2 1

18. Students need to be more aware of their academic
abilities. 4 3 2 1

19. Students need to learn about necessary training and
skills for various jobs. 4 3 2 1

20. Students need to explore their interests. abilities, and
aptitudes. 4 3 2 1

21. Students need to understand the effect work has on life. 4 3 2 1

22. Students need to know about jobs that are available
to them. 4 3 2 1

23. Students need to know how to apply for a job. 4 3 2 1

24. Students need to know what to say and do during
a job interview. 4 3 2 1

25. I need to know more about reviewing and interpreting
student records. 4 3 2 1

26. I need to know more about referring students to the
counselor. 4 3 2 1

27. I need to know more about making student referrals
for special education classes. 4 3 2 1

28. I need to know more about curriculum development
and how to be more involved in this process. 4 3 2 1

29. I need help in communicating with parents more
effectively. 4 3 2 1

30. I think the school needs to provide more opportunities
for staff development via in-service workshops. 4 3 2 1

Figure 7.7. Needs assessment survey for students in grades 4 through 6: A sample.

Deer Run Elementary School

Counseling Program Needs Assessment Survey
Grades 4, 5, and 6
Student Survey

The counseling staff and the Counseling Program Advisory Team of the Mill Creek School District need your help in identifying the needs of students in our school. Your responses on this survey will be of great value in helping develop a counseling program that can more effectively meet your needs as a student.

Instructions: Circle your grade level. After reading each statement carefully, circle the number that corresponds most closely to your need. Respond to each statement honestly—no one will have access to your responses. When everyone has completed the survey, your teacher will collect them and send them to the counseling center.

Figure 7.7. Continued.

Deer Run Upper Elementary School Needs Survey
Student Version

Circle your grade level: 4   5   6

Instructions: Circle the number you feel best fits the level of need for each of the following statements.

	high			low
1. I need to learn how to feel better about myself.	4	3	2	1
2. I need to understand myself better.	4	3	2	1
3. I need to learn how to tell others how I feel.	4	3	2	1
4. I need to better understand the effects of alcohol and drugs.	4	3	2	1
5. I need to understand death.	4	3	2	1
6. I need to understand separation and divorce.	4	3	2	1
7. I need to know more about the needs and feelings of others.	4	3	2	1
8. I need to know how others see and feel about me.	4	3	2	1
9. I need to understand better what my parents expect of me.	4	3	2	1
10. I need help getting along better with members of my family.	4	3	2	1
11. I need help in participating in social groups that are satisfying to me.	4	3	2	1
12. I need to become aware of different kinds of social groups.	4	3	2	1
13. I need to know more about school policies and rules.	4	3	2	1
14. I need to understand how I am progressing in each class and how I can improve my work.	4	3	2	1
15. I need to know how to study better.	4	3	2	1
16. I need to become more aware of the services available through the counseling program.	4	3	2	1

Figure 7.7. Continued.

17. I need to do more work at school and at home.   4 3 2 1

18. I need to know more about possible careers and the world of work.   4 3 2 1

19. I need to know what I must do to prepare for work I want to do in the future.   4 3 2 1

20. I need to learn more about the difference between work time and free time.   4 3 2 1

Figure 7.8. Needs assessment survey for students in grades 2 and 3: A sample.

Deer Run Elementary School

Counseling Program Needs Assessment Survey
Grades 2 and 3
Student Survey

Read by the teacher to the students: Today we will be helping the counselors know more about how to help students in our school.

Instructions (read by the teacher): Do not write your name on the paper. As I read each statement, circle either "yes" or "no" depending upon what you think or how you feel about each statement. If you do not understand a statement, raise your hand and I will explain what the statement means. Respond to each statement according to how you think or feel, not how you believe others would want you to answer.

When we have completed the survey. I will collect the surveys and take them to the counseling center.

Figure 7.8. Continued.

Deer Run Lower Elementary School Needs Survey
Student Version

Circle your grade: 2   3

Instructions: Listen to each statement and then circle either "yes" or "no."

1. I need to learn how to feel good about myself.	yes no
2. I need to understand myself and the things I do.	yes no
3. I need to learn how to tell others how I feel.	yes no
4. I want to learn about alcohol and drugs.	yes no
5. I need to know what to do if someone I love dies.	yes no
6. I need to learn about divorce.	yes no
7. I think kids need to learn to be nicer to others.	yes no
8. I would like to get along better with others my age.	yes no
9. I want to get along better with my parents.	yes no
10. I want to get along better with my brothers and sisters.	yes no
11. I need to learn how to make friends.	yes no
12. I want to learn how to share with others.	yes no
13. I need to know more about school rules.	yes no
14. I need to know what my grades mean.	yes no
15. I want to learn to read faster.	yes no
16. I want to learn how my school counselor can help me.	yes no
17. I need to learn how to be a helper at school and at home.	yes no
18. I want to learn about the different jobs in our community.	yes no
19. I need to find out why people work.	yes no
20. I think kids need to learn more about hobbies, games, and fun activities.	yes no

Figure 7.9. Needs assessment survey for students in grades K and 1: A sample.

Deer Run Elementary School

Counseling Program Needs Assessment Survey
Grades Kindergarten and 1
Student Survey

Read by the teacher to the students: Today we will be completing a survey that will help the counselors know more about how to help you.

Instructions (read by the teacher): Do not write your name on the survey. As I read each statement, circle either "yes" or "no" depending upon what you think or how you feel about each statement. If you do not understand a statement, raise your hand and I will explain what the statement means. Respond to each statement according to how you think or feel, not how you believe others would want you to answer.

When we have finished, I will collect the surveys and take them to the counseling center.

Figure 7.9. Continued.

Deer Run Primary Elementary School Needs Survey
Student Version

Circle your Grade: K   1

Instructions: Listen to each statement and then circle "yes" or "no."

1.	I need to learn to feel good about myself.	yes	no
2.	I need to understand why I do things.	yes	no
3.	I need to learn how to tell others when I am sad.	yes	no
4.	I want to learn about drugs and alcohol.	yes	no
5.	I want to learn about what to do if someone I love dies.	yes	no
6.	I want to learn what to do if my mom or dad moves away from home.	yes	no
7.	Kids in my class need to learn how to be nice to each other.	yes	no
8.	I need to learn to get along with the kids in my class.	yes	no
9.	I want to learn how to get along better with my mom and dad.	yes	no
10.	I need to learn how to get along better with my brothers and sisters.	yes	no
11.	I need to learn how to make friends.	yes	no
12.	I need to learn to share my toys with other kids.	yes	no
13.	I need to learn to understand classroom rules.	yes	no
14.	I want to know what my grades mean.	yes	no
15.	I need to learn to be a better reader.	yes	no
16.	I would like to know the school counselor.	yes	no
17.	I need to learn to be a helper at school and at home.	yes	no
18.	I want to know what my parents do at work.	yes	no
19.	I need to know why people work.	yes	no
20.	I want to know how to play more games.	yes	no

Figure 7.10. Needs assessment survey for parents of elementary school students: A sample.

Deer Run Elementary School

Counseling Program Needs Assessment Survey
Parent Survey

The counseling staff and the Counseling Program Advisory Team of the Mill Creek School District request your assistance in identifying the needs of students, parents, teachers/administrators, and the community in our school district. With your help, the counseling staff will be able to address priority needs more directly.

Instructions: After completing the requested information at the top of the survey, read each statement carefully and then circle the number you believe most closely corresponds to the need. When you have completed the survey, please return it to the counseling center. You may deliver it personally, mail it, or send it to school with your child. Please respond to this survey within a week. Thank you for your interest and assistance.

/

Figure 7.10. Continued.

Deer Run Elementary School Needs Survey
Parent Version

**Circle the grade level of your child
or children:**   K   1   2   3   4   5   6

Instructions: Circle the number you feel best fits the level of need for each of the following statements.

		high			low

1. My child needs to develop self-awareness and
    self-acceptance.   4 3 2 1

2. My child needs to understand him- or herself.   4 3 2 1

3. My child needs to learn to share his or her feelings
    with others.   4 3 2 1

4. My child needs to be educated about drugs and
    alcohol and their effects.   4 3 2 1

5. My child needs to learn how to deal with death
    and dying.   4 3 2 1

6. My child needs to learn how to deal with parental
    divorce.   4 3 2 1

7. Children need to learn how to be more accepting
    and kinder to others.   4 3 2 1

8. My child needs to learn to communicate with peers. 4 3 2 1

9. My child needs to be more aware of parental
    expectations.   4 3 2 1

10. My child needs to learn to get along better with
    family members.   4 3 2 1

11. My child needs to learn how to make and keep friends. 4 3 2 1

12. My child needs to learn to share with others.   4 3 2 1

13. My child needs more information about school
    policies and rules.   4 3 2 1

14. My child needs to learn how school learning applies
    to the non-school environment.   4 3 2 1

Figure 7.10. Continued.

15. My child needs to improve his or her study habits.   4 3 2 1

16. My child needs to learn more about available
    counseling services.   4 3 2 1

17. My child needs to learn to help more at home.   4 3 2 1

18. My child needs to learn about various jobs in the
    community.   4 3 2 1

19. My child needs to understand the effect work has
    on one's life.   4 3 2 1

20. My child needs to learn about leisure activities.   4 3 2 1

21. I need to know more about the counseling program.   4 3 2 1·

22. I need more information regarding educational
    opportunities for my child.   4 3 2 1

23. I need to learn more effective parenting skills.   4 3 2 1

24. I need to visit with the counselor concerning my
    child's needs.   4 3 2 1

25. I need to develop a better relationship with my
    child's teachers.   4 3 2 1

Figure 7.11. Needs assessment survey for teachers and administrators of elementary schools: A sample.

Deer Run Elementary School

Counseling Program Needs Assessment Survey
Teacher and Administrator Survey

The counseling staff and the Counseling Program Advisory Team of the Mill Creek School District request your assistance in identifying the needs of students, parents, teachers/administrators, and the community. With your help, the counseling staff will be able to address priority needs more directly.

Instructions: After completing the requested information at the top of the survey, read each statement carefully, then circle the number you believe most closely corresponds to the need. When you have completed the survey, return it to the counseling center. Please respond to this survey within five days. Thank you for your interest and assistance.

Figure 7.11. Continued.

Deer Run Elementary School Needs Survey
Teacher and Administrator Version

Circle the grade level(s) you teach or supervise: **K 1 2 3 4 5 6**

Instructions: Circle the number you feel best fits the level of need for each of the following statements.

		high		low

1. Students need help in gaining awareness of their feelings about themselves. 4 3 2 1

2. Students need help in understanding themselves and others. 4 3 2 1

3. Students need to learn to deal with their feelings. 4 3 2 1

4. Students need to know about the dangers of drugs and alcohol. 4 3 2 1

5. Students need to know how to deal with death and dying. 4 3 2 1

6. Students need to learn how to deal with parental divorce. 4 3 2 1

7. Students need to learn to be more accepting and kinder to their peers. 4 3 2 1

8. Students need to learn to communicate more effectively with their peers. 4 3 2 1

9. Students need to learn to communicate more effectively with their parents. 4 3 2 1

10. Students need to learn how to get along better with their families. 4 3 2 1

11. Students need to learn how to deal with peer pressure. 4 3 2 1

12. Students need to learn how to work within the social group. 4 3 2 1

13. Students need to know more about the school policies and rules. 4 3 2 1

14. Students need to understand the importance of making good grades. 4 3 2 1

Figure 7.11. Continued.

15. Students need help in learning study skills.   4 3 2 1

16. Students need to learn more about services offered
    by the counselor.   4 3 2 1

17. Students need to learn to help their teachers and
    parents.   4 3 2 1

18. Students need to learn about different jobs in the
    community.   4 3 2 1

19. Students need to understand why people work.   4 3 2 1

20. Students need to learn new hobbies and games which
    prepare them for enjoying leisure time activities.   4 3 2 1

21. I need to know more about reviewing and interpreting
    student records.   4 3 2 1

22. I need to know more about referring students to the
    counselor.   4 3 2 1

23. I need to know more about making student referrals
    for special education classes.   4 3 2 1

24. I need to know more about curriculum development
    and how to be more involved in this process.   4 3 2 1

25. I need to know how to more effectively meet the
    needs of my students.   4 3 2 1

26. I need to know more about classroom discipline
    models.   4 3 2 1

27. I need help in communicating with parents more
    effectively.   4 3 2 1

28. I need to develop a better relationship with the
    counselor.   4 3 2 1

29. I need help learning to develop and conduct guided
    classroom activities.   4 3 2 1

30. I think the school needs to provide more opportunities
    for staff development via in-service workshops.   4 3 2 1

Figure 7.12. Needs assessment survey for business and industry: A sample.

Mill Creek Community Business and Industry Needs Survey

The counseling staff and the Counseling Program Advisory Team of the Mill Creek School District request your assistance in identifying the needs of students, parents, teachers/administrators. and the community. With your help, the counseling staff will be able to address priority needs more directly.

Instructions: Please indicate the nature of your business or industry activity: Retail trade, Manufacturing, Hospitality, Health care, Government, Agriculture, Personal Service (cosmetology, child care), etc.: _____

Circle the number you feel best fits the level of need for each of the following statements. Persons seeking employment need:

		high			low
1.	Knowledge of appropriate dress for interviews.	4	3	2	1
2.	Knowledge about the importance of accuracy and neatness when completing job applications.	4	3	2	1
3.	Knowledge and skills for interviewing.	4	3	2	1
4.	Importance of team skills.	4	3	2	1
5.	Importance of attendance at work.	4	3	2	1
6.	Ability to get along with fellow workers.	4	3	2	1
7.	Understanding of problem solving strategies.	4	3	2	1
8.	Willingness to take initiative on the job.	4	3	2	1
9.	Technical skills with computers or programmable machines.	4	3	2	1

Figure 7.13. Interview type of survey: An example.

**Mill Creek Counseling Program
Needs Assessment Survey**

**Students, Parents, Teachers, Administrators,
and Other Community Members**

The Mill Creek School District counseling and administrative staff and the Counseling Program Advisory Team need your help identifying the needs of students, parents, school personnel, and the community which can be served by the school counselors and the counseling program. Your responses to the following questions will be of great value in helping us identify needs as well as indicating those areas with which you are satisfied. For each statement, please indicate whether you think there is a

1. **High need:** Students are not receiving help in this area and there is a definite need for counselor attention.

2. **Medium need:** Students are receiving some help in this area, which should be continued.

3. **Low need:** Students have received adequate help in this area or do not need help in this area.

Instructions for Interviewer: After reading the explanation of the purpose of the interview and the rating criteria, read each statement, circle the response, and record any comments.

Figure 7.13. Continued.

Mill Creek School District Needs Assessment Survey

Check all items that apply: ___ Student ___ Parent
___ Teacher ___ Administrator
Grade level _____
___ Community Member

Please rate the need for students to do the following:

Personal, Behavioral, and Emotional Skills Statement	**H**	**M**	**L**
1. Develop self-awareness and self-acceptance	3	2	1
2. Learn to deal with their feelings in effective ways	3	2	1
3. Know how to plan and use time well	3	2	1
4. Be educated about drugs and alcohol and their effects	3	2	1
5. Be taught sex education in school	3	2	1
6. Develop good decision-making skills	3	2	1
7. Develop a sense of responsibility	3	2	1
8. Learn to express needs, ideas, and feelings	3	2	1

Social Actions and Skills

9. Become aware of personal expectations and attitudes of social groups and situations	3	2	1
10. Understand and interact with peers	3	2	1
11. Learn about love, marriage, and family interaction	3	2	1
12. Become more aware of responsibilities in the home	3	2	1
13. Understand and interact with adults	3	2	1
14. Adjust to and become knowledgeable about the school environment	3	2	1

Educational Performance and Future Planning

15. Become aware of available counseling services	3	2	1
16. Improve their study skills and habits	3	2	1
17. Apply school learning to non-school environment	3	2	1

Figure 7.13. Continued.

Lifestyle and Career Future

18. Explore a wide range of career options   3 2 1

19. Explore a suitable career choice compatible with the
    student's interests, abilities, and attitudes   3 2 1

20. Identify requirements for career choices and to prepare
    for career goals   3 2 1

21. Understand the effect work has on one's life   3 2 1

Figure 7.14. Needs rankings for a senior high school, listed by stakeholder groups, as determined from survey data.

Mill Creek School District Counseling Program

Needs Assessment Rankings
Senior High School (Grades 10 through 12)

*S*tudent   *T*eacher   *P*arent   *A*dministrative

Personal, Behavioral, and Emotional Skills Rankings	S	T	P	A
1. Explaining self-awareness and self-acceptance	6	2	5	6
2. Understanding themselves and their actions	4	3	4	4
3. Being aware of their strengths and weaknesses	5	4	6	5
4. Being more honest with others about how they feel	8	1	7	8
5. Learning to deal with feelings in effective ways	2	7	3	3
6. Learning to deal with death and dying	7	8	8	7
7. Learning to deal with divorce	1	6	1	1
8. Education about drugs and alcohol and their effects	3	5	2	2
Social Actions and Skills Rankings				
9. Sharing needs, ideas and feelings with others	4	2	1	2

Figure 7.14. Continued.

10. Learning to stand up for themselves in a group	1	1	2	1
11. Learning to be more tolerant of people whose views, appearance, or actions differ from their own	7	3	3	3
12. Learning about love, marriage, and family living	2	4	8	6
13. Learning to get along better with family members	3	6	3	5
14. Learning how to help parents accept friends	6	8	5	7
15. Becoming more aware of responsibilities at home	8	7	7	8
16. Learning to work with counselors and administrators	5	5	6	4

Educational Performance and Future Planning Rankings

17. Becoming aware of available counseling services	6	1	6	6
18. Providing information about graduation requirements	7	2	7	7
19. Improving study skills and habits	8	3	8	5
20. Developing test-taking skills	2	4	1	2
21. Improving the ability to concentrate	1	5	3	1
22. Understanding standardized test scores	4	6	4	8
23. Applying school learning to non school environment	3	7	2	3
24. Providing information about educational alternatives after high school	5	8	5	4

Lifestyle and Career Future Rankings

25. Explore interests, abilities and aptitudes	6	2	5	8
26. Training, skills, and future of certain occupations	2	3	8	2
27. Information on the job market	4	4	1	5
28. Pursuing a definite career plan	5	6	3	4
29. Preparation for selecting career goals	1	7	6	6
30. Identify requirements for career choices	3	8	4	3
31. Provisions for on-the-job experience in career interest area	8	1	2	1
32. Understanding the effect work has on one's life	7	5	7	7

Figure 7.15. Needs for a senior high school, listed by the advisory team, following tabulation of results from a needs assessment survey.

Mill Creek Senior High School Ranked Needs Ranked by the Advisory Team

Personal, Behavioral, and Emotional Skills

1. Learning to deal with divorce

2. Education about drugs and alcohol and their effects

3. Understanding themselves and their actions

4. Learning to deal with feelings in effective ways

Social Actions and Skills

1. Learning to stand up for themselves in a group

2. Sharing needs, ideas, and feelings with others

3. Learning to be more tolerant of people whose views, appearance or actions differ from their own

Educational Performance and Future Planning

1. Developing test-taking skills.

2. Improving the ability to concentrate

3. Applying school learning to non school environment

Lifestyle and Career Future

1. Provisions for on-the-job experience in career interest area

2. Information on job market

3. Training, skills, and future of certain occupations

Figure 7.16. Needs rankings for a junior high school, listed by stakeholders, as determined from survey data.

Mill Creek School District
Counseling Program Needs Assessment Rankings

School Level: Cherokee Falls Junior High School (Grades 7 through 9)

*S*tudent   *T*eacher   *P*arent   *A*dministrative

Personal, Behavioral, and Emotional Skills Rankings	S	T	P	A
1. Understand how feelings affect behavior	5	6	6	4
2. Learn how to express feelings more honestly	3	4	2	5
3. Understand death	4	5	3	6
4. Understand separation and divorce	1	2	4	2
5. Understand the effects of drugs and alcohol	2	1	1	1
6. Learn to be responsible for own actions	6	3	5	3

Social Actions and Skills Rankings

	S	T	P	A
7. Learn to stand up for self in a group instead of being a wallflower	3	1	1	3
8. Learn to be more tolerant of people with differing views	5	2	6	2
9. Learn how to get along better with members of the opposite sex	1	3	5	5
10. Learn to understand adults better	6	5	3	6
11. Understand parental expectations	2	4	2	4
12. Talk more with the counselor	4	6	4	1

Educational Performance and Future Planning Rankings

	S	T	P	A
13. Learn about services available through the counseling program	1	2	3	1
14. Learn study skills	3	1	2	2
15. Learn how things studied in school will be useful outside of school	5	5	6	5

Figure 7.16. Continued.

16. Learn which courses are required and which are
    electives   6 6 5 6

17. Learn how to take tests   2 3 1 3

18. Learn about ability to do school work   4 4 4 4

Lifestyle and Career Future Rankings

19. Learn about what workers must learn to do for jobs
    I might like   2 4 2 3

20. Learn to make plans for developing abilities in my
    career interest areas   6 1 5 4

21. Understand more about the effect work has on life   3 5 1 1

22. Find out what jobs are available locally   5 2 6 6

23. Learn how to apply for a job   1 3 3 2

24. Learn what to do and say in a job interview 4 6 4 5

Figure 7.17. Needs for a junior high school, listed by the advisory team, following tabulation of results from needs assessment survey data.

Cherokee Falls Junior High School Needs Ranked by the Advisory Team

Personal, Behavioral, and Emotional Skills

1. Need to better understand the effects of alcohol and drugs

2. Need to understand separation and divorce

3. Need to learn how to express feelings more honestly

Social Actions and Skills

1. Need to stand up for self in a group instead of being a follower all the time

2. Need to better understand parent expectations

3. Need to know how to get along better with members of the opposite sex

Educational Performance and Future Planning

1. Need to become more fully aware of the services available through the counseling program

2. Need to improve study habits

3. Need to learn how to take tests

Lifestyle and Career Future

1. Need to know how to apply for a job

2. Need to understand more about the effect work will have on my life

3. Need to know more about what workers must learn to do for jobs I might like

Figure 7.18. Needs rankings for an elementary school, listed by stakeholder groups, determined from survey data.

Mill Creek School District Counseling Program Needs Assessment Rankings

School Level: Deer Run Elementary School (Grades K through 6)

| | *S*tudent | *T*eacher | *P*arent | *A*dministrative |

Personal, Behavioral, and Emotional Skills Rankings	S	T	P	A
1. Develop self-awareness and self-acceptance	3	1	1	1
2. Understanding themselves	6	5	6	6
3. Learn to share feelings with others	5	6	2	5
4. Education about drugs and alcohol and their effects	4	4	3	3
5. Understand death and dying	2	3	4	2
6. Learn how to deal with parental divorce	1	2	5	3
Social Actions and Skills Rankings				
7. Learn to be more accepting and kinder to others	4	3	2	2
8. Learn to communicate with peers	5	5	6	4
9. Become more aware of parent expectations	2	4	1	3
10. Learn to get along better with family members	6	6	4	6
11. Learn how to make and keep friends	1	1	3	1
12. Learn to share with others	3	2	5	5
Educational Performance and Future Planning Rankings				
13. More information about school policies and rules	3	1	4	4
14. Learn how school learning applies to the non-school environment	4	4	2	3
Lifestyle and Career Future				
17. Learn to help more at home	4	4	1	4
18. Learn about various jobs in the community	1	3	3	1
19. Understand the effect work has on one's life	3	1	2	3
20. Learn about leisure activities	2	2	4	2

Figure 7.19. Needs for an elementary school, listed by the advisory team, using needs assessment survey data.

Deer Run Elementary School Ranked Needs Ranked by the Advisory Team

Personal, Behavioral, and Emotional Skills

1. Learning to feel better about self (self-awareness and self-acceptance)

2. Learning to understand death and dying

Social Actions and Skills

1. Learning how to make and keep friends (participating in satisfying social groups)

2. Understanding parental expectations

Educational Performance and Future Planning

1. Becoming more aware of the services available through the counseling process

2. Improving study habits

3. Understanding how school learning applies to the non-school environment

Lifestyle and Career Future

1. Learning about various jobs in the community

2. Understanding the effect work has on one's life

3. Learning about leisure activities

Figure 7.20. Goals, objectives, and activities from four domains for an elementary school: A sample.

Deer Run Elementary School Goals, Objectives, and Activities, Developed by the Counseling Staff and the Advisory Team

Personal, Behavioral, and Emotional Skills

First Priority Need: To learn how to feel better about myself.

Goal: To help students develop more positive feelings about themselves.

Management Objectives

1. By October 30th, one teacher in-service will have been held to share ideas with teachers on increasing student positive feelings about self as evidenced by an agenda and teacher evaluations on file in the counselor's office.

2. By November 18th, all K-6 classrooms will have started a series of guided activities and discussions on enhancing self-esteem as evidenced by a calendar of classroom visits in the counselor's office.

3. By April 1st, individual consultations with all teachers will have been completed to offer assistance, support, encouragement, and share ideas about increasing student positive feelings toward self as evidenced by the counselor's calendar of appointments with teachers.

Outcome Objectives

1. By the end of the school year, K-6 students will show a 3% gain in pre- and post-test comparisons on a self-concept inventory.

Strategies/Activities

1. Counselors conduct teacher in-service to share ideas on how to improve student feelings about self.

   1a. Activities and Discussion Topics: Personal-1 in Elementary Counseling Curriculum Guide.

   1b. Teacher in-service evaluation: Personal-2 in Elementary Counseling Curriculum Guide.

Figure 7.20. Continued.

2. Implement classroom activities on self-esteem enhancement, grades K-6.

   2a. *Description of Materials:* Personal-3 in Elementary Counseling Curriculum Guide.

Social Actions and Skills

First Priority Need: To understand better how to make and keep friends.

Goal: To help students with participation in satisfying social groups.

Management Objectives

1. By September 1st, the counselor in consultation with K-3 teachers will have identified students who are in need of special assistance in social play as evidenced by a list of identified students in the counselor's office.

2. By October 1st, K-3 teachers and the counselor will have completed a plan for classroom groups designed to encourage appropriate social behavior in all students as evidenced by a plan on file in the counselor's office.

3. By November 30th, students in grades 4-6 will have been involved in three classroom guided activities and discussions on the topic, "Getting and Keeping Friends" as evidenced by an agenda for the classroom visits and a calendar of completed visits.

4. By December 1st, small group discussions designed to assist students with peer group participation will be scheduled with fifth- and sixth-grade students as evidenced by a list of students and dates and times for meetings.

Outcome Objectives

1. After participating in classroom activities and guided discussions, fifth- and sixth-grade students will show a 10% larger selection of favorite friends as measured by pre- and post-comparisons on a sociometric list of favorite friends.

2. After participating in planned activities designed to improve participation in social groups, students in grades K-6 will obtain higher teacher ratings on social adjustment when compared to pre-test ratings.

Figure 7.20. Continued.

Strategies/Activities

1. Students identified by teachers as needing special assistance in social play see the counselor for individual counseling assessment.

2. Teachers lead a series of six classroom guided activities in all K-3 classrooms.

   2a. Activities: Social- 1 in Counseling Curriculum Guide.

   2b. Students having difficulty in classroom groups participate in six counselor led small group sessions.

   2c. Follow group formation format: Social-2 in Counseling Curriculum Guide.

   2d. Suggested activities: Social-3 in Counseling Curriculum Guide.

   2e. Students having difficulty dealing with group participation are counseled individually.

3. Grades four through six teachers conduct three classroom activities and discussions on "Getting and Keeping Friends."

   3a. Activities: Social-4 in Counseling Curriculum Guide.

4. Students identified by teachers as needing additional assistance in forming friendships participate in six weeks of small group counseling.

   4a. Follow group formation format: Social-2 in Counseling Curriculum Guide.

   4b. Suggested activities: Social-5 in Counseling Curriculum Guide.

5. Pre- and post-inventory, "List of favorite friends": Social-6 in Counseling Curriculum Guide.

6. Social Adjustment Checklist: Social-7 in Counseling Curriculum Guide.

Educational Performance and Future Planning

First Priority Need: To become more aware of the services available through the counseling program.

Figure 7.20. Continued.

Goal: To increase student awareness of the services available through the counseling program.

Management Objectives

1. By September 1ˢᵗ, the counselors will review two commercially available packages for informing students of the services available from the counseling program as evidenced by staff evaluation notations and a recommendation for purchase on file.

2. By October 15ᵗʰ, a plan for implementing an internal information program which includes classroom visits, announcements, and printed material will be initiated with all K-6 students as evidenced by a schedule of events on file.

Outcome Objective

1. After all efforts to inform students of services available from the counseling program have been completed, 80% of the students will be able to correctly answer five out of eight questions about the services provided by the counselors.

Strategies/Activities

1. Counseling staff reviews two commercial programs for informing students and parents of available counseling services.

   1a. A program is selected and purchased. The program is on file in the Media Center.

   1b. Counselors present the program at the October Deer Run Elementary PTO meeting.

2. Counselors visit each classroom and provide information about counseling services.

   2a. Discuss services for students. Activities: Educational- 1 in Counseling Curriculum Guide.

   2b. Counseling Services Questionnaire: Educational-2 in Counseling Curriculum Guide.

Lifestyle and Career Future

First Priority Need: To learn about various jobs in the community.

Goal: To improve students' understandings of the types of workers in their community.

Figure 7.20. Continued.

Management Objectives

1. By November 1st, the counselors will have conducted an assessment meeting with K-3 teachers to determine the nature and extent of efforts presently underway to help students learn of workers in their community as evidenced by a list of all teaching units and activities.

2. By November 1st, counselors will have conducted assessment meetings with 20% of the fourth- through sixth-grade students to determine the nature and specifics of their need for knowledge of careers and the world of work as evidenced by a listing of jobs they wish to learn about.

3. By December 1st, a plan for improving K-6 student understandings of possible careers and the world of work will have been completed as evidenced by a written plan on file.

Outcome Objective

1. After participating in planned activities, students will be able to correctly answer 85% of the items on a counselor/teacher made test of knowledge about possible careers and the world of work.

Strategies/Activities

1. Counselors and teachers of grades K-3 meet to determine what is currently being taught in class about careers and to determine what is needed.

    la. All teachers share their activity plans and organize a common plan for each grade level.

2. Classrooms are randomly selected (grades 4-6) for completing the "World of Work" Assessment: Career-1 in Counseling Curriculum Guide.

3. All K-6 classes observe "Career Week" the second week of February.

    3a. Activity plans: Career-2 in Counseling Curriculum Guide.

4. "World of Work Test of Knowledge": Career-3 in Counseling Curriculum Guide.

Chapter 8

EVALUATION

Planning for evaluation is part of a comprehensive plan from the beginning. Planning for evaluation allows the advisory team and the professional counseling staff to accomplish three main purposes.

1. It provides the data needed for accountability. Having a design for collecting that data anticipates the question, "Are you doing what you planned to do?" Generally, accountability data permit easy response to questions about the operational aspects of the program, and provides information about the performance of the counselors and other persons working on the various guidance strategies.

2. The evaluation plan provides a means by which adjustments and changes can happen during implementation of the plan. The actual effects of every activity and strategy cannot be fully anticipated, and usually some activities are just not effective for a variety of reasons. An evaluation plan provides for regular checkups and allows for continuous improvement during the implementation phase of the plan.

3. A well-conceived evaluation lets the advisory team know whether the goals of the counseling and guidance program were realized. In the final analysis, a good evaluation plan makes it possible to answer the most fundamental questions: Did we accomplish the mission? Did we reach our goals? Did we meet the identified needs? Summative evaluation measures the extent to which the desired ends are reached.

THE ADVISORY TEAM IN EVALUATION

The advisory team is responsible for developing the evaluation plan, reviewing and revising the plan during implementation, and completing revisions in the plan after the implementation cycle. The advisory team will decide how often to review data about program effectiveness; however, some kind of formalized review should be conducted on an annual basis, as well (formative evaluation). Annual reviews serve as interim evaluations and offer good opportunities for making adjustments.

Some districts choose to do less formal evaluation reviews by keeping the focus on formative and continuous revisions for three years prior to a major evaluation review. It is probably appropriate for most schools to make annual reports based on all data available and to expect a major redesign of the program plan after conducting needs analysis in cycles of five or six years (summative evaluation).

Major demographic changes such as rapid growth or decline in population may necessitate more frequent needs assessment. However, for most school districts a five- or six-year cycle of assessing needs is adequate. The schedule selected for evaluation will be determined by variables such as the size and complexity of the program plan, the size of the school, the resources available, and the experience of the counseling staff and advisory team. From year to year, advisory teams and counseling staffs become more accomplished in gathering data, revising the plan, and knowing how to determine what is really important.

In the final analysis, a good and effective needs-based program plan will reduce needs. Therefore, the needs assessment conducted for the five- or six-year evaluation cycle may provide additional evidence of program quality, particularly when needs are found to move to a lower priority.

TYPES OF EVALUATION

Accountability Logs

Accountability is simply a way of documenting what has been done. Everything we do as counselors—from showing up for work, to spending money wisely, to being available for students—can be a source of accountability data. Having a plan for gathering accountability data also permits counselors to monitor who, how, what, and when actions were taken. In addition, continuous accounting provides evidence of inadvertent diversions of time and energy to activities outside the approved plan. Accountability data should be compiled regularly, reviewed by the counseling staff, and reported to the appropriate administrative office and members of the advisory team. At a minimum it should contain a summary of:

1. the number of student contacts during the reporting period by grade level,

2. the number of teacher and parent contacts, and

3. the number of referrals to outside agencies.

Some counselors maintain simple logs of kinds and numbers of contacts each day and total them for each week. Items listed on the counselor's calendar could be totaled daily as well as weekly. Another approach is to create a preset list of categories of activities—such as individual counseling, small group counseling, classroom guidance, parent contact, telephone contact, and test interpretation—for keeping a tally. You simply place tally marks beside the listed activity. Each day a total can be determined and the day totals added for the week. You also can list categories of activities or tasks and assign symbols or time slots for the tally marks to show how much time was given to each task.

Accountability is a way of verifying the nature and amount of activity devoted to the many tasks of the counselor. With some thought and shared ideas, a simple way of recording information for reports, as well as internal and external public relations, can improve perceptions and provide data for both formative and summative evaluations.

Formative Evaluation

Formative evaluation is the process of collecting and reviewing data during the implementation phase for purposes of continuously shaping or improving the program. It requires systematically gathering evidence that can be used as a basis for adjustment and revision of individual components of the program at any time. Formative evaluation is aimed at improving the functions, strategies employed, or the expertise of individuals so that the effectiveness of the counseling and guidance program can remain focused on accomplishing the established mission and goals.

A review of formative data permits continuous program revision aimed at more effective use of strategies and resources and thereby increases the likelihood of reaching the goals. Formative evaluation is not aimed at changing the goals themselves. Interim formative evaluation should show what changes are needed in strategies or direction, current policies, and practices. *Goals are only changed after completion of an implementation cycle.*

For example, if evidence indicates that students are uninterested or unaffected by a specific approach to improving communication with parents, another approach should be tried as soon as possible. Continuing with an ineffective strategy obviously is counterproductive. It is important to avoid becoming a slave to the plan, especially when there is evidence of needed change.

You should document any adjustments and discuss all such changes; they also should be incorporated into records for the advisory committee's review upon revision of the plan at the end of the implementation cycle, when new goals may be in order. Often, adjustments are needed to ensure that pursuit of the goals remains the top priority and is continuous. Formative evaluation supports the notion that if something doesn't seem to be working, it should be changed now rather than later.

A formal record of adjustments made should be included in monthly reports. Even informal notes are useful and positive when periodic reviews are made. To some extent, every strategy is one of trial and error, and much can be learned from any reliable evidence of whether a particular strategy is positive or negative.

Summative Evaluation

Summative evaluation is the final compilation of all evidence of program effectiveness. Answering the question, "Did we reach the goals we set?" is essential if the advisory team is to evaluate the effectiveness of the program plan and create an improved design for the next five- or six-year cycle. Data generated by the individual outcome objectives help in deciding the level of effectiveness in the program design. Once the data have been collected and organized, the advisory team must examine, analyze, and interpret the results. The data must be analyzed in the context of the knowledge and experience of the professional counseling staff. A critical examination of formal and informal data is needed to obtain maximum benefit from the evaluation and to do the best job possible in redesigning for the next five- or six-year cycle.

Needs-Based Evaluation

Completing a needs assessment at the end of the five- or six-year planning cycle can provide some evidence of program effectiveness. However, you should interpret such evidence with caution; any conclusions you reach should have support from other data sources. It is useful to compare the relative position of priority needs found on the first assessment (at the beginning of planning) with those found on the second assessment (at the end of the five- or six-year cycle).

Theoretically, a perfectly effective counseling and guidance program that is planned around priority needs will reduce those needs. It is possible then to find in the second needs assessment indicators of program effectiveness, particularly if the order of priority or ranking has changed or the original need is no longer a priority. This approach, however, is more useful in theory rather than in practice because of the many variables that can make such an interpretation problematic.

For example, changes in economic conditions may affect families and communities and so influence the needs identified in the second round of assessment. Another difficulty is the possibility that some needs have moved up in priority because of increased awareness resulting from program effectiveness. This higher-priority status may be attributable to the positive effects of program outcomes. Clearly, variables known to have an impact on such results should be carefully considered by the advisory team. When changes are measured, a difference in priority needs simply serves as an indicator of where resources should go during the next program cycle.

If data and careful analysis indicate that the program was effective in reducing needs, a decision will be necessary as to what changes should be made in the program design. Perhaps existing resources can be committed to some other priority need. On the other hand, perhaps no changes should be made because the original need was critical and any such changes might risk the gains that have been achieved. For example, the second needs assessment might show low priority for a need in the category of *conflict resolution skills*. And the evidence found in the summative evaluation data might show that students are indeed experiencing less conflict and are handling conflicts more appropriately. However, rather than reallocate resources on conflict resolution, the advisory team might want to continue the current strategies for conflict resolution because the original need was in the context of violence and injury to students and teachers. In other words, the risk of returning to the former state of affairs might be so strong that no change is the best course of action in planning for the next five- or six-year cycle.

On the other hand, if the second needs-based analysis shows clearly that the availability of information and assistance on college applications and scholarships is adequate, due to available technology, and that fewer sessions with the counselor are necessary for students, then more of the counselor's time can be allocated elsewhere. Institutionalization of certain strategies—such as the use of technology, volunteers, other community resources and participation by other staff in the guidance functions—may permit counselors to deliver more intensive services to another priority need.

The sample K–12 evaluation in Figure 8.1 shows how an interim evaluation enables annual adjustments in the planned program, provides strong evidence of progress, and forms the basis for communicating with school and community stakeholders. This evaluation is based on the goals, objectives, and strategies developed in Chapter 7. Figure 8.1 includes a list of the priority needs, a restatement of the goals and objectives, and an evaluation summary for all three school levels. Next, it gives an overall statement of evaluation, which would have been approved by the advisory team. The last section lists recommendations for specific changes in the plan, along with the attendant proposed administrative actions.

A major benefit of performing needs-based evaluations is the sense of accomplishment and success that can contribute to higher morale and satisfaction of the counseling staff. Many counselors feel discouraged because they lack evidence that the work they perform results in concrete gains for the publics they serve. Evaluations based on objectives provide evidence of progress, while documentation of the nature, frequency, and duration of counselor contacts with students, staff, and parents provides evidence of the level of involvement and number of hours committed to the various activities of the counseling program by counselors, teachers, administrators, student workers, parents, and community volunteers.

(Continued on page 152.)

Figure 8.1. Evaluation for all three school levels: A sample.

Mill Creek School District

Sample Evaluation for Senior High School

Needs

The following priority needs were identified by the advisory team:

1. Learning to deal with divorce

2. Learning to stand up for themselves in a group

3. Developing test-taking skills

4. Provisions for student on-the-job experience in a selected career interest area

Goals

The following goals were established by the advisory team:

1. To increase knowledge and skills needed for dealing with divorce.

2. To improve students' ability to stand up for themselves in groups.

3. To improve student test-taking skills.

4. To provide on the job experience in career interest areas.

Personal, Behavioral, and Emotional Skills: Goal 1

Evaluation Summary

Four activities were scheduled and designed to improve students' knowledge of and skills for dealing with divorce. A general school assembly–attended by students in the 10th, 11th, and 12th grades–was held on October 3. Dr. Divorce Counselor from the Mill Creek Mental Health Center discussed the problems, issues, anxieties, and adjustments most commonly experienced by parents, children, and adolescents following a family divorce. Dr. Counselor's presentation was followed by a panel discussion with parents and their children who have had a divorce experience. The counseling staff publicized classroom follow-up discussions, group counseling, and individual counseling. Three counseling groups, eight classroom follow-up discussions, and 20 individual sessions were arranged within three days after the assembly.

Figure 8.1. Continued.

Outcome Objective 1-a: After attending a one-hour school assembly program and participating in three classroom discussions on divorce, 80% of the students will be able to describe the common feelings, issues, problems, and coping skills associated with divorce as evidenced by written assignments collected in English classes.

Results: Of the 100 students who turned in brief papers on divorce to four English teachers on December 1ˢᵗ, 85% received grades of B or better for the portion judged on accuracy of information. The objective was met.

Outcome Objective 1-b: After participating in 12 weeks of small-group counseling on the theme of divorce, 75% of the students participating will report improved ability to deal with the feelings, issues, and problems of divorce as evidenced by student verbal statements and notes made by the counselor during the last group session.

Results: Notes and comments from students completing 12 weeks of group counseling on divorce issues show that 70% reported they are better able to make the adjustments and cope with their own feelings as a result of group counseling. The objective was not met.

Outcome Objective 1: After participating in individual and/or group counseling sessions, students will show a decreased level of anxiety as evidenced by pre- and post-test comparisons on a stress checklist and an increase in understanding of divorce as evidenced by pre- and post-test responses on an inventory addressing feelings about divorce.

Results: Pre- and post-test results for those students who completed six or more individual counseling sessions and eight or more group counseling sessions showed reduced anxiety as measured by the stress checklist and an increase in understanding of divorce as measured by the feelings about divorce inventory. These data are supported by a 15% improvement in grades for the grading period immediately following counseling. The objective was met.

Social Actions And Skills: Goal 2

Evaluation Summary

Brief interviews were held with a 2% sample of students in order to identify specific peer group pressures experienced by students. The list developed through the interviews was used to plan an assertiveness training group, which began on Nov. 21 and continued until Christmas

Figure 8.1. Continued.

break. Eighteen students participated in five hours of training. Concurrently, four evening meetings were held for parents and students on strategies to deal with peer pressure. Students who needed additional help were encouraged to participate in group counseling and individual counseling. Three counseling groups continued for eight weeks and involved 36 students. A "Speak for Yourself" club started with 10 members on February 12, and grew to 18 members by the end of April.

Outcome Objective 2-a: After six months of operating the programs listed above, 10% more students will be involved in appropriate extracurricular activities and 10% fewer students will be involved in disciplinary proceedings as evidenced by rosters and logs of events.

Results: Attainment of these outcomes is inconclusive at this date. Further evaluation will be completed when six months have passed.

Outcome Objective 2-b: After participating in assertiveness training for six weeks, students will show a 50% gain in correct responses on an assertiveness communication inventory.

Results: Students participating in assertiveness training showed a 65% gain in correct responses on a pre/post-inventory of assertiveness communications. This objective was met.

Educational Performance and Future Planning: Goal 3

Evaluation Summary

Work on a short course for students on test-taking skills was completed on October 1. Seven teachers completed a 45-minute in-service training session on the short course and agreed to conduct at least three short courses for students before the March statewide testing date.

Students were given reports of progress on teacher-made tests for each week and each grading period after completing the course.

Outcome Objective 3-a: After completing a short course on test-taking skills and participating in a discussion group for three weeks, 70% of the students will show a one-half letter grade improvement as evidenced by grades received for the second-quarter grade reports.

Results: By May 1, 107 students had completed the course. Seventy students had a 25% gain in test scores. This effort exceeded expectations and, even though it ran behind schedule, it will be continued and expanded next year.

Figure 8.1. Continued.

Lifestyle and Career Future: Goal 4

Evaluation Summary

Agreements for shadowing opportunities were completed with 33 employers, and two mini-workshops were held on career decision making. A total of 28 students attended these workshops.

Outcome Objective 4-a: After completing a mini-workshop on career decision making and three shadowing experiences, students will report a 2-point increase in certainty about the appropriateness or inappropriateness of their present career choices as evidenced by pre- and post-ratings on a counselor-developed Likert-type scale.

Results: Pre- and post-activity comparisons show a change of 1.5 points for students completing the mini-workshops. This objective was not met.

Outcome Objective 4-bc: After completing the activities in the career decision-making mini-workshop, participants will (1) have selected three shadowing options related to their current career choices as evidenced by completed student choice sheets on file in the counselor's office, and (2) show by written description how their abilities and aptitudes, interest patterns, values, and lifestyle choices relate to their career selections.

Results: Of the students completing the mini-workshops, 98% selected three shadowing options and were able to show how their selections were appropriate for their own career choices. Interests, values, aptitudes, and lifestyle choices were shown to be compatible with the shadowing options selected. These objectives were met.

Overall Evaluation for Mill Creek Senior High School

The high school (grades 10 through 12) counseling program appears to have operated in an exceptionally fine manner to accomplish the goals that had been previously established. The staff worked systematically toward each goal and objective. The achievement of the outcome objectives suggests a high level of quality involvement with students, staff, and parents. An evaluation of progress toward each of the above goals and objectives will be completed at the end of each of the next three years.

Figure 8.1. Continued

Mill Creek School District

Sample Evaluation for Cherokee Falls Junior High School

Needs

The following priority needs were identified by the advisory team:

1. To better understand the effects of alcohol and drugs.
2. To stand up for themselves in groups instead of being followers all the time.
3. To become more fully aware of the services available through the counseling program.
4. To know how to apply for a job.

Goals

The following goals were established by the advisory team:

1. To improve students' understanding of the effect of alcohol and drugs.
2. To improve students' ability to stand up for themselves in peer groups.
3. To increase student awareness of services available through the counseling program.
4. To improve the job application abilities of students in grades 7 through 9.

Personal, Behavioral, and Emotional Skills: Goal 1

Evaluation Summary

All activities were completed as planned in the management objectives. The results obtained from the planned measures in the outcome objectives suggest that progress was made in informing students about the effects of alcohol and drugs. However, it is not clear from the evidence that students are reporting less use of drugs and alcohol. Pre- and post-measure comparisons of reported use remained at 13% for the total student body. The objectives were not met.

Figure 8.1. Continued

Social Actions and Skills: Goal 2

Evaluation Summary

Classroom discussions and a peer training group were held. Data collected during the classroom discussions showed that students could role-play and specifically identify the behavioral choices necessary to stand up for themselves. The objectives were met.

Educational Performance and Future Planning: Goal 3

Evaluation Summary

Classroom meetings were held to describe the services available from the counseling staff. A checklist completed by students at the end of the meetings showed that 87% had learned about at least three new services offered by the counselors. This objective was met.

Lifestyle and Career Future: Goal 4

Evaluation Summary

All activities planned to meet Goal 4 have not been completed. However, after completing the activities to date, an improvement in job application skills and performance on a video-taped interview were achieved. All planned activities for reaching Goal 4 will be continued through the first three months of next year. This objective was not met.

Overall Evaluation for Cherokee Falls Junior High School

The program showed strength in informing students about the effects of alcohol and drugs and helping students to stand up for themselves in groups. Students are better informed about counseling services and have learned new skills in applying for jobs and interviewing.

Mill Creek School District

Sample Evaluation for Deer Run Elementary School

Needs

The following priority needs were identified by the advisory team:

1. To learn how to feel better about myself.

2. To understand better how to make and keep friends.

Figure 8.1. Continued

3. To become more aware of the services available through the counseling program.

4. To know more about possible careers and the world of work.

Goals

The following goals were established:

1. To help students develop more positive feelings about themselves.

2. To help students with participation in satisfying social groups.

3. To increase students' awareness of the services available through the counseling program.

4. To improve students' understanding of the types of workers in their own community.

Personal, Behavioral, and Emotional Skills: Goal 1

Evaluation Summary

All classroom activities and consultations with teachers were held as planned. Counselors worked beyond the plan to provide resource materials for teachers on self-concept and to assist them in making the classroom climate a positive force for student learning. Pre- and post-test results on the self-concept inventory showed a 2.5% gain during the first year. This objective was not met. A gain of 3% may have been an unrealistic expectation.

Social Actions and Skills: Goal 2

Evaluation Summary

Teacher reports and the results obtained from the sociometric measures indicate some progress toward Goal 2; however, a continued effort to improve social skills of K–3 students is needed to reach the goal. This objective was not met.

Educational Performance and Future Planning: Goal 3

Evaluation Summary

Counselors reviewed three available commercial packages for informing students about counseling services, and selected one. A plan for

Figure 8.1. Continued

classroom visits, announcements, and printed material was completed as scheduled. By the end of the year, 85% of the students correctly answered six of the eight questions concerning services offered by the counselors. The objective was met.

Lifestyle And Career Future: Goal 4

Evaluation Summary

The planned activities of teachers indicated that considerable effort was already underway in classrooms. The counselors worked to help the teachers arrange field trips and resource speakers for classrooms and to systematically cover career information about several new community jobs. Student performance on a teacher/counselor-made test showed excellent knowledge about community jobs. This objective was met.

Overall Evaluation for Deer Run Elementary School

The elementary program showed strength in working with teachers, informing students about the counseling program, and assisting in career education efforts.

Mill Creek School District

General Evaluative Summary, K–12

The evaluation data gathered at the end of one year of program implementation suggest that significant progress has been made toward achieving the goals associated with the identified needs. Administrative evaluation of staff performance and the results obtained from public opinion questionnaires support the notion that the staff and community are better informed about the counseling program.

The advisory team commends the counseling staff, administrators, and board of education for undertaking this effort. Continued efforts over the next five years will bring the counseling program full circle to the next major planning cycle and make possible one of the best counseling programs in the state.

Recommendations

1. Continue all planned activities as scheduled next year.
2. Conduct annual interim evaluations for years 2, 3, and 4.

Figure 8.1. Continued.

3. During year 5 begin planning for a major revision of the plan which includes updated needs assessment surveys.

4. Work to plan more drug and alcohol information programs at the elementary school level.

5. Introduce the "Speak for Yourself" club at the junior high school level.

6. Work with the student body leadership and parent teacher organization to further impact the use of drugs and alcohol by students.

7. Work on improving school and classroom climate at all levels.

8. Consider more counselor efforts to be resource persons for administrators and teachers.

ADMINISTRATIVE EVALUATION

In addition to evaluating program effectiveness, the administration must evaluate counselors and the program. Administrative evaluation provides a means for decisions on the employment, tenure, and merit raises for each counselor. All too often, counselor evaluations follow a process similar to those for teachers. In some districts the same forms are used. But this method may result in inadequate or inaccurate evaluation. If the advisory team has produced a quality plan with sound program evaluation built in, it remains necessary to document the effectiveness of each counselor. Sample survey and evaluation forms are included in this chapter to encourage advisory teams to develop specific personnel evaluation procedures, forms, and methods that will improve evaluation outcomes. Counselors who perform poorly or deliver poor service to students, teachers, and parents should be readily identified, and appropriate steps for remediation or removal should be taken. Systematically gathering evaluation data based on established standards of performance protects individual counselors, administrators, and the profession. It is less than adequate to have the assistant principal sit in on a classroom guidance session and rate the counselor using a teacher evaluation form.

Gathering evaluation data may provide direct feedback on the opinions of various stakeholder groups on the operation and effectiveness of the counseling program plan. Opinions of consumer groups may not provide accurate information when only individual or small samples are surveyed. A large sample of parent, teacher, and student population groups can provide clear clues about problem areas as well as outstanding performance of both individual counselors and the counseling staff as a whole.

We have included sample evaluation inventories to suggest how questionnaires may be structured to gather feedback on the performance of counselors (see Figures 8.2 through 8.5). These instruments have been used successfully by many school districts. We suggest the advisory team include specific recommendations for administrative evaluation in the final written plan. Figures 8.2, 8.3, and 8.4 show how information and opinions can be gathered from various consumer populations to help administrators evaluate the counseling program and its staff. Such opinions from various stakeholders are a valuable aid to administrators in assessing the visibility, involvement, professional development, and public relations efforts of counselors. The counselor's self-inventory and the evaluation by the principal, as outlined in Figure 8.5, could be used to help the counselor and administrator with annual evaluation conferences and serve as a basis for annual improvement goals.

Evaluation must hold a place of importance alongside all other components of the plan. The long-term aspects of comprehensive planning require that accountability, personnel, operation, and quality receive thorough evaluation on a regular basis. Operation and outcomes can be readily evaluated by scanning the evidence collected when objectives have been reached. Judgments made after a review of the program's outcomes by professional staff and advisory team can provide evidence of quality. As long as evaluation—both formal and informal—is continuous and based on accurate data, improvement is possible. Evaluation should lead to recommendations for improvements, refinements, and changes.

SUMMARY

A really good needs-based program plan and evaluation should provide a sharply defined and specific focus on the population, need, and strategy. Such a focus allows targeted adjustments once the first planning, implementation, and evaluation cycle has been completed. Long-term institutionalized planning is essential if school counseling is to realize its full potential and we are to have maximum effect on the students we serve. Evaluation must be continuous and extensive. We must learn to clearly define what we are working to accomplish and find accurate and reliable means of measuring the extent to which we achieve those ends.

Clearly, in the day-to-day rush of responding to all the demands made on our time by those we serve, it is difficult to stand back in an analytical way and examine hard evidence about our work. Nevertheless, if we practice relentlessly and learn continuously, we will find a better path to the quality and excellence we seek as we strive to bring the learning and benefits we intend to our students.

Figure 8.2. Counselor evaluation form to be completed by the school building administrator: A sample.

Administrator Survey

School: _____ **Date:** _____

Directions: For each item circle the number that best reflects the effectiveness of the counselor assigned to your school.

A. Effectiveness with Students

To what extent does the counselor

		Always				Never
1.	motivate students to seek counseling when needed?	4	3	2	1	0
2.	demonstrate sensitivity to students' feelings?	4	3	2	1	0

Figure 8.2. Continued.

3. promote good rapport with students?   4 3 2 1 0

4. help students with personal as well as educational
    and vocational problems?   4 3 2 1 0

5. have a positive image with students?   4 3 2 1 0

6. function effectively as a resource consultant
    to students?   4 3 2 1 0

B. Effectiveness with Teachers

To what extent does the counselor

1. demonstrate sensitivity to the role and problems
    of the teacher?   4 3 2 1 0

2. cooperate willingly with all school personnel?   4 3 2 1 0

3. communicate easily and effectively with teachers?   4 3 2 1 0

4. demonstrate receptiveness to teacher comments
    and suggestions?   4 3 2 1 0

5. promote good rapport with teachers?   4 3 2 1 0

6. function effectively as a resource consultant to
    teachers?   4 3 2 1 0

7. provide relevant feedback to the teacher?   4 3 2 1 0

C. Effectiveness with the Administration

To what extent does the counselor

1. understand the concerns of the administration?   4 3 2 1 0

2. demonstrate a professional rationale for his or
    her counseling approach?   4 3 2 1 0

3. cooperate with administration regarding
    development of the counseling program?   4 3 2 1 0

4. promote good rapport with administration?   4 3 2 1 0

5. attend to, follow through, and report back on
    administration referrals?   4 3 2 1 0

6. function effectively as a resource consultant to
    administrators?   4 3 2 1 0

Figure 8.2. Continued.

D. Effectiveness with Parents

To what extent does the counselor

	Always				Never
1. understand parental concerns?	4	3	2	1	0
2. promote free and easy communication between school and home?	4	3	2	1	0
3. provide time for parents?	4	3	2	1	0
4. have a professional image with parents?	4	3	2	1	0
5. attend to parental referrals?	4	3	2	1	0
6. follow through with parental needs?	4	3	2	1	0

Please respond to the following questions. If additional space is needed, use the other side of this page.

I would like to see this counselor (or these counselors) continue working in my school. (Explain) _____

_____

_____

What are the strengths of the counseling program at your school?_____

_____

_____

What are suggestions for improving the counseling program at your school?_____

_____

_____

_____

Figure 8.3. Counselor evaluation form to be completed by parents: A sample.

Parent Survey

School:_____ Date: _____

Please circle the following items from 5 to 1 (5 indicating strongly agree; 1 indicating strongly disagree) to best reflect your concepts about the counselor in your child's school.

1. The counselor is a valuable resource at my child's
   school.   5 4 3 2 1

2. The availability of individualized counseling is a
   valuable resource to promote successful social and
   emotional development.   5 4 3 2 1

3. Group counseling activities (e.g., substance abuse
   prevention, self-esteem building) have helped my
   child develop necessary and important life skills. 5 4 3 2 1

4. Counselors are able and willing to give parents
   useful information in successfully dealing with
   their children.   5 4 3 2 1

5. I like the idea of being able to consult with a
   counselor about my child's progress.   5 4 3 2 1

6. My school's counselor has provided me with
   information I can use in helping my child with his
   or her emotional and educational development.   5 4 3 2 1

Respond to the following questions. If additional space is needed, use the other side of the page.

I would like to see this counselor (or these counselors) continue working in my school. (Explain)_____

_____

_____

_____

Figure 8.3. Continued.

What are the strengths of the counseling program at your school?_____

_____

_____

_____

What are some suggestions for improving the counseling program at your school?_____

_____

_____

_____

Figure 8.4. Counselor evaluation form to be completed by teachers: A sample.

Teacher Survey

School: _____ Date: _____

Directions: On each item circle the number that best reflects the effectiveness of the counselor assigned to your school.

A. Effectiveness with Pupils

To what extent does the counselor

		Always				Never
1. motivate students to seek counseling when needed?		4	3	2	1	0
2. demonstrate sensitivity to students' feelings?		4	3	2	1	0
3. promote good rapport with students?		4	3	2	1	0
4. help students with personal as well as educational and vocational problems?		4	3	2	1	0
5. have a positive image with students?		4	3	2	1	0
6. function effectively as a resource consultant to students?		4	3	2	1	0

B. Effectiveness with Teachers

To what extent does the counselor

1. demonstrate sensitivity to the role and problems of the teacher? 4 3 2 1 0

2. cooperate willingly with all school personnel? 4 3 2 1 0

3. communicate easily and effectively with teachers? 4 3 2 1 0

4. demonstrate receptiveness to teacher comments and suggestions? 4 3 2 1 0

5. promote good rapport with teachers? 4 3 2 1 0

6. function effectively as a resource consultant to teachers? 4 3 2 1 0

7. provide relevant feedback to the teacher? 4 3 2 1 0

Figure 8.4. Continued.

Please respond to the following questions. If additional space is needed, use the other side of this page.

I would like to see the counselor (or these counselors) continue working in my school. (Explain)_____

_____

_____

_____

What are the strengths of the counseling program at your school?_____

_____

_____

_____

What are suggestions for improving the counseling program at your school?_____

_____

_____

_____

Figure 8.5. Counselor self-inventory and evaluation by principal: A sample.

Counselor's Self-Inventory and Evaluation by Principal

Counselor:_____ School: _____

Grade: _____ Date: _____

The counselor and the principal should each complete a separate copy of this form. Ratings should be compared and discussed during an annual evaluation review.

Rating:

1. Indicates an outstanding level of performance, well above that expected for the position.

2. Indicates that a broad range of performance is considered to meet the requirements of the position.

3. Indicates a performance level that the evaluator and the evaluatee will work together to improve.

4. Indicates an unacceptable performance level (substantiated by written conference reports).

Note: Narrative comments must be written in support of any item rated 3 or 4 by either evaluatee or evaluator. N/A may be used if the item is not applicable to the evaluatee.

Effectiveness as a Person

_____ 1. Relates effectively with others.

_____ 2. Exhibits sensitivity, empathy, and acceptance necessary for establishing rapport.

_____ 3. Functions in an organized manner.

_____ 4. Respects the individual.

_____ 5. Has a sense of humor.

_____ 6. Is respected.

Figure 8.5. Continued.

_____ 7. Exhibits poise and stability.

_____ 8. Is professionally ethical.

Effectiveness with Students

_____ 1. Motivates students to seek counseling.

_____ 2. Is sensitive to students' feelings.

_____ 3. Has a good rapport with students.

_____ 4. Helps students with personal as well as educational and vocational problems.

_____ 5. Has a positive image among students.

_____ 6. Functions effectively as a resource consultant to students.

_____ 7. Uses instructional and student personnel services in a sensitive and appropriate manner in dealing with student problems.

_____ 8. Encourages students to use other service personnel when appropriate and actively assists in the accomplishments of the objectives.

Effectiveness with Teachers

_____ 1. Is sensitive to the role and problems of the teacher.

_____ 2. Cooperates willingly with all school personnel.

_____ 3. Communicates easily and effectively with teachers.

_____ 4. Is receptive to teacher comments and suggestions.

_____ 5. Has a good rapport with teachers.

_____ 6. Functions effectively as resource consultant to teachers in matters of curriculum, student activities, and human interaction as well as the concerns for psychological climate surrounding learning experiences.

Effectiveness with the Administration

_____ 1. Understands the role and concerns of the administration.

_____ 2. Has a professional rationale for his or her counseling approach.

Figure 8.5. Continued.

____ 3. Cooperates with the administration regarding development of the counseling program.

____ 4. Has a good rapport with administration.

____ 5. Attends to, follows through, and reports back on administration referrals.

____ 6. Functions effectively as a resource consultant to the administration in matters of curriculum, student activities, and human interaction as well as the concerns for psychological climate surrounding learning experiences.

Effectiveness with Parents

____ 1. Is understanding of parental concerns.

____ 2. Promotes free and easy communication between school and home.

____ 3. Is available to parents.

____ 4. Has a professional image among parents.

____ 5. Attends to parental referrals.

____ 6. Follows through with parents in reducing crises and responding to their needs for counselor services.

Effectiveness in the Profession

____ 1. Takes pride in being a member of the counseling profession.

____ 2. Continues to involve him- or herself in activities to improve professional skills.

Chapter 9

THE COUNSELING PROGRAM ACTIVITY GUIDE

Rebecca Groves Brannock, Ph.D., LPC
Assistant Professor, Department of Psychology and Counseling
Pittsburg State University

The development of a counseling program activity guide serves a number of purposes, including these:

1. It provides instructions and activities for classroom teachers.

2. It allows counselors and teachers to evaluate activities and to change or alter those that are not effective.

3. It provides for easy review of classroom and small group activities by parents and others.

4. It contains in outline form a complete view of what activities counselors and teachers are conducting.

5. It facilitates the addition of new activities as further needs are identified.

An activity guide should be developed for each school level. A large three-ring binder is the best type of cover, since activities can be added or deleted easily. The guide should include an introduction that explains the guide's purpose and how to use it and a section for activities addressing personal, social, educational, and career needs.

A sample activity guide is included in this chapter. The goals, objectives, and activities addressed are included in the needs assessment surveys from Chapter 7. Naturally, your guide will be more extensive and include specific activity worksheets and other information unique to your school district. The activities included here cover top priority needs in each of the four areas (personal, social, educational, and career) for each of the three school levels (elementary, junior high, and senior high). We have also included information on publishers and costs for the resources recommended. You should review all advertisements and catalogs you receive in the mail, visit book exhibits at state and national counseling conferences, attend conference presentations, and talk to other counselors about materials they are using before developing your own activity guide.

An activity guide is an important document to have available whenever a parent or community member questions the focus of your counseling activities. Most people questioning counseling program activities don't understand what you are presenting in the classroom or in small groups. Allowing them to review the activities alleviates most of their concerns.

MILL CREEK SCHOOL DISTRICT COUNSELING PROGRAM ACTIVITY GUIDE

Compiled by Mill Creek School Counseling Staff

Dr. Linda Listener
Advisory Committee Coordinator

The School Board of Mill Creek

Forest T. Woods, President
Jena Jump, Vice President
I. Will Tellem, Treasurer
Sydney Speaker, Member
Joe Followman, Member
Mary May, Member

Dr. J.J. Leader
Superintendent of Schools
Mill Creek School District
Fall Valley Administration Building
2000 E. 20th
Mill Creek, USA

ACKNOWLEDGMENTS

We would like to thank the following Mill Creek School District counselors, teachers, and advisory team members for sharing their time and energy to make this guide possible.

Linda Listener, Mill Creek Senior High Counselor
John I. Care, Cherokee Falls Junior High Counselor
Jill Loving, Deer Run Elementary Counselor
Edna Educator, Mill Creek Senior High Counselor
Barry Good, Cherokee Falls Junior High Teacher
Mary Printer, Deer Run Elementary Teacher
Ralph Respect, Cherokee Falls and Deer Run Parent
Donna Doright, Mill Creek Senior High Student

Other School Staff Credits

• Computer assistance: Judy Type's Office Machines Class

• Editorial assistance: Dean Writer's Advanced Writing Class

We also would like to thank all the students and parents of the Mill Creek School District. By working as a team, our youth of today will become better prepared leaders tomorrow.

PREFACE

This counseling activity guide was developed after an advisory team was appointed and trained, a needs assessment was conducted, needs were ranked and prioritized, and program goals and objectives were developed. This has been a joint effort for school staff, advisory team members, students, and the counseling staff.

Our youth of today encounter many difficult situations that require them to make wise decisions, to deal with negative peer pressure, and to solve their own problems. We believe the social and emotional growth of our students is important to their educational growth. We must help our students develop healthy relationships with themselves and others, learn to communicate effectively with peers and adults, and take responsibility for their actions, both positive and negative.

The activities in this guide will allow students to participate in classroom activities led by counselors and teachers, in counselor-led small groups addressing a variety of topics, and in individual counseling sessions when there is a need.

This guide is not a finished product. As further needs are identified, activities will be added to address them. We simply want to suggest here preventive strategies that may help eliminate the need for crisis interventions.

MILL CREEK SENIOR HIGH SCHOOL

Goals, Objectives, and Activities

Personal, Behavioral, and Emotional Skills

Priority need: Learning to deal with divorce

Goal: To increase coping skills for dealing with parents' divorce

Management Objectives

1. By October 15th a panel of alumni students whose parents are divorced will speak to all sophomore students in English II classes.

2. By October 25th interested students may elect to participate in small group counseling sessions for coping with divorce.

3. By November 1st small group counseling sessions will begin and will be conducted weekly until the Christmas holiday.

4. After the Christmas holiday, follow-up individual counseling sessions will be conducted to ascertain whether coping skills are being used.

Outcome Objectives

1. After hearing a panel of students discuss their feelings about being from divorced families, 80% of the students will be able to describe the feelings, concerns, and coping skills most commonly associated with being from a divorced home, as indicated by a reaction paper written in English classes.

2. Upon completion of eight weeks in small group counseling sessions for coping with divorce, 75% of the students

will report improved ability to deal with their feelings and issues surrounding divorce, as evidenced by verbal comments made in the final group counseling session.

3. After participating in follow-up individual counseling sessions, students will show a decreased level of anxiety associated with divorce, as indicated by verbal comments made to the counselor and by pre- and post-test responses on the checklist "My Feelings About Divorce."

Strategies/Activities

1. A panel of alumni students whose parents are divorced share their experiences to all English II classes.

2. Individuals self-refer themselves for participation in small group counseling sessions to cope with divorce.

3. Small group sizes will be limited to 10 students per group, with school counselors facilitating the groups at different times: before school, during advisory periods, and after school.

4. Group sessions will be held weekly for 50 minutes over an eight-week period.

5. Group sessions will follow an eight session format as outlined in *School-Based Divorce Groups* (Haezebrouck & Summerell, 1989).

6. Pre- and post-test "My Feelings About Divorce": Personal-1.

7. Follow-up with individual counseling sessions after the Christmas holiday, continuing to meet with students regularly who are still having difficulty coping. Personal-1

"My Feelings About Divorce"

Students should indicate whether they feel the following statements are true (t) or false (f).

_____ 1. Problems, fears, and worries will go away if kids don't talk about how they feel to others and pretend everything is okay.

_____ 2. Kids can change their parents' minds about getting a divorce.

_____ 3. People should never divorce, no matter what the reason.

_____ 4. It is impossible for people to be friends once they divorce.

_____ 5. People whose parents are divorced often worry about the success of their own marriage.

_____ 6. Children should be forced to visit the parent they don't live with, even if they don't want to.

_____ 7. When kids lives with one parent, it means they are taking sides against the other parent.

_____ 8. Parents who get a divorce don't love their kids.

_____ 9. Children in a family should have "veto power" if they don't like the person their parent wants to marry.

_____ 10. Kids from divorced families will never be as happy as kids from "real," married families.

_____ 11. It is normal for kids to be nervous, upset, and worried about the future during their parents' divorce.

_____ 12. Most of the kids who get into trouble at school have divorced parents.

____ 13. The courts always award physical custody to mothers.

____ 14. Kids who live with a single parent have more responsibilities and stress than kids from married families.

____ 15. Kids should hide the truth from their friends about their parents' divorce; it's something to be ashamed of.

Source: Haezebrouck and Summerell (1989).

MILL CREEK SENIOR HIGH SCHOOL

Social Actions and Skills

Priority need: Learning to get along better with family members

Goal: To improve relationships with parents by increasing communication skills with them

Management Objectives

1. By January 15th students will view the video *The Power of Choice: Communicating with Parents* (Pritchard, 1994) during junior-level speech classes and will practice role-playing various scenarios.

2. By January 16th students will complete the assessment "Parents Relationship Scale" and will discuss in small groups the issues that present problems with their parents.

3. By January 17th students will write "Imagine If" letters to their future children about their expectations as parents.

4. By January 20th students will complete a homework assignment designed to increase communication with their parents.

5. By February 1ˢᵗ parents will be invited to participate in parenting classes on increasing communication skills with their teenagers.

Outcome Objectives

1. After viewing *The Power of Choice: Communicating with Parents*, 80% of the students will be able to explain and role-play techniques for getting their parents to listen to and understand them.

2. After completing the "Parents Relationship Scale," 90% of the students will know where they stand in terms of relationships with their parents.

3. After writing "Imagine If" letters, 75% of the students will be able to compare their expectations as future parents to their parents' current expectations.

4. Upon completion of the homework assignment to interview parents about issues of concern when they were teenagers, 80% of the students will have an opportunity to discuss various topics with their parents.

5. After parents are given the opportunity to participate in parenting classes, 75% will report improved communication with their teenagers.

Strategies/Activities

1. Eleventh-grade speech students will view the 30-minute video, *The Power of Choice: Communicating with Parents*. Afterward, students will role-play various scenarios, with half portraying parents and the other half as themselves.

2. Juniors will complete the "Parents Relationship Scale" and score the instrument for immediate feedback. The scale is available in *Self-Exploration Inventories* by Lee and Pulvino (1993).

3. Students will be given the opportunity to write imaginary letters to their future children, including their expectations as future parents.

4. Students will be assigned homework that will involve interviewing their parents: Social-1.

5. Parenting classes will be held for parents who would like to increase communication skills with their teenagers. The hour-long classes will be held on four consecutive Tuesday evenings at 7 P.M. Resource materials will be pulled from *Parenting Teenagers: Systematic Training for Effective Parenting* by Don Dinkmeyer (1989).

Social-1
Parent Interview Questions

Name of Student: _____

Parent Interviewed: _____

Date of Interview: _____

1. As a teenager, what was your relationship with your parents like? _____

   _____

   _____

2. At what age were you allowed to date? _____

   _____

3. Did you have a curfew as a teenager? _____

   _____

4. What disagreements did you have with your parents? _____

   _____

   _____

5. What household chores were you responsible for? _____

   _____

6. What did you most like about being a teenager? _____

   _____

   _____

7. What did you least like about being a teenager? _____

_____

_____

8. What concerns or issues did you have when you were a teenager? _____

_____

_____

9. How would you describe me to your future grandchild? _____

_____

_____

_____

10. How would you explain what being a parent is like? _____

_____

_____

_____

Source: Questions were developed by Rebecca Brannock, Ph.D. (1997).

MILL CREEK SENIOR HIGH SCHOOL

Educational Performance and Future Planning

Priority need: Improving study skills and habits.

Goal: To improve study skills.

Management Objectives

1. By November 1st all sophomores in World History classes will be given the inventory "How Do You Study?" to assess their study habits.

2. By November 3rd students will receive training in a series of workshops on improving study skills.

3. By November 15th any students who would like to receive peer tutoring help may sign-up and begin meeting with a peer tutor before school.

Outcome Objectives

1. After taking the "How Do You Study?" inventory, 80% of the students will be familiar with their strengths and weaknesses in their study habits.

2. Upon completion of study skills training sessions, 75% of the student will indicate an improvement in their study habits, as reflected by responses given on the post-test.

3. Of the students who elected to receive peer tutoring help, 80% will report an increase in grades at the end of the quarter.

Strategies/Activities

1. Sophomore students will complete the "How Do You Study?" inventory from *Self-Exploration Inventories* (Lee & Pulvino, 1993).

2. Sophomores will receive training over a three-day series of workshops on improving study skills. Topics covered will include taking class notes, reading textbooks, managing time and environment, and preparing for tests. Resource materials are provided by ACT's *Study Power* (Brown, 1987).

3. Sophomores who need additional peer tutoring help will receive services before school from the high school's peer tutors.

MILL CREEK SENIOR HIGH SCHOOL

Lifestyle and Career Future

Priority need: Career preparation

Goal: To increase job-seeking skills to secure future employment

Management Objectives

1. By April 1st all senior high students in English IV classes will take the "Job Seeking Attitude Scale" assessment, discuss pointers for completing job applications, and complete an application form properly.

2. By April 2nd English IV students will receive tips on writing a resume and will develop a personal resume.

3. By April 3rd seniors in English IV will view the video *Job Interview Skills* (Sunburst Communications, 1993a) and will discuss the do's and don'ts of job interviewing.

4. By April 4th community members will be invited into the English IV classes to conduct mock interviews with students in front of their classmates.

Outcome Objectives

1. After taking the "Job Seeking Attitude Scale," 80% of the students will be aware of their attitudes to improve their approaches to job seeking. Additionally, 80% will be able to properly complete a job application.

2. After hearing tips on developing a resume, 80% of the students will be able to create their own personal resumes.

3. After viewing the video on job interview skills, 80% of the students will be aware of the do's and don'ts of job interviewing.

4. After observing mock interviews in class, 90% of the students will receive immediate feedback from prospective employers about the strengths and weaknesses of classmates' job interviewing skills.

Strategies/Activities

1. Seniors will complete the inventory, "Job Seeking Attitude Scale" in *Self-Exploration Inventories* (Lee & Pulvino, 1993). Students also will receive pointers on completing job applications from *An Introduction to Job Applications* (Farr, 1994).

2. Students will write their own personal resumes using pointers and samples from *The Resume Solution* (Swanson, 1995).

3. Students will view the 30-minute video *Job Interview Skills.*

4. Various community members will be invited to conduct mock interviews during class. Four students will be selected per class period to be interviewed. Students will submit job applications and resumes prior to the interviews and will dress appropriately.

CHEROKEE FALLS JUNIOR HIGH SCHOOL

Goals, Objectives, and Activities

Personal, Behavioral, and Emotional Skills

Priority need: To understand death

Goal: To cope with the loss of a loved one

Management Objectives

1. By March 1st 9th-grade vocational classes will view a video on grief to understand its impact on individuals experiencing loss and will discuss various losses in people's lives. A guest speaker from a local hospice will discuss the grieving process.

2. By March 2nd 9th-grade students will hear a story "The Amethyst Ring" and will discuss its impact and meaning in small groups.

3. By March 7th any student wishing to participate in group counseling sessions on coping with the loss of a loved one may volunteer.

Outcome Objectives

1. After viewing the video *A Child's View on Grief* (Wolfelt, 1990) and hearing the guest speaker, 80% of the students will have a clearer understanding of grief and will be able to identify various losses people may experience as well as ways to cope with those losses.

2. Once students have heard the story "The Amethyst Ring," 70% will be able to discuss the meaning of the story and relate to some of the losses in their own lives.

3. After participating in six small group counseling sessions for coping with the loss of a loved one, 80% of the stu-

dents will be able to use coping techniques in dealing with their losses.

Strategies/Activities

1. Students in 9ᵗʰ-grade vocational classes will view the video *A Child's View of Grief,* made available by funeral homes. A guest speaker from a local hospice will discuss typical grief reactions as well as ways to cope during a difficult time.

2. Students will hear the story "The Amethyst Ring" and discuss questions in small groups: Personal-2. A resource to use with students in dealing with loss is *Windows: Healing and Helping Through Loss* by Mary Joe Hannaford and Michael Popkin (1992).

3. Students who volunteer may participate in six small group counseling sessions on coping with the loss of a loved one. A resource that includes complete session-by-session plans is *Group Counseling for School Counselors: A Practical Guide* by Greg Brigman and Barbara Earley (1991).

Personal-2

Source: Hannaford and Popkin (1992) is an excellent resource that can help children deal with loss. "The Amethyst Ring" is one of the heartwarming stories included. After reading the story, Hannaford and Popkin suggest addressing the following questions:

• What was the major loss?

• What was the first reaction?

• What other reactions did you notice?

• Who comforted her?

• Besides the ring and the money, what else was lost?

• What do you think was gained from the experience?

CHEROKEE FALLS JUNIOR HIGH SCHOOL

Social Actions and Skills

Priority need: Learn to be more tolerant of people with differing views

Goal: To learn to use negotiation in dealing with peer pressure

Management Objectives

1. By October 1st all 7th-grade health classes will hear several high school students talk about their experiences of resisting peer pressure in junior high and currently.

2. By October 2nd 7th-graders will receive training in negotiating peer pressure situations. The students will then role-play the skills in class.

3. By October 3rd students will participate in several in-class activities to practice skills negotiating with others.

4. By October 10th any student who is interested in participating in the peer helper program at the junior high school will be encouraged to apply.

Outcome Objectives

1. After hearing high school students talk about personal experiences with peer pressure, 70% of the students will be aware of the need to avoid giving in to peer pressure.

2. After being trained in the skills necessary to negotiate peer pressure situations, 80% of the students will be able to role-play these skills.

3. Upon further practice, 80% of the students will be able to use their skills to negotiate and compromise with others in given situations.

4. After hearing about the peer helper program at the junior high school, 50% of the students will apply to become peer helpers.

Strategies/Activities

1. Students in 7th grade will hear high school students share personal experiences in dealing with peer pressure, to realize they are not alone when confronted with various situations.

2. Students will be trained in the skills necessary to negotiate peer pressure. The resource used Begun (1996).

3. All 7th-grade students will continue practicing skills learned through various role-play situations and activities: Social-2.

4. Any 7th-grade students who are interested in participating in the peer helper program will complete an application form to apply. A resource to help establish a peer helper program in schools is *Peers Helping Peers* (Tindall & Salmon-White, 1990).

Social-2

Source: Begun (1996). Permission is given for individual classroom teachers to reproduce the activity sheets and illustrations for classroom use.

A Family Curfew Compromise

Directions: Discuss the following situation with each member of your family and write down their responses in the space below.

Your friends say they can stay out as late as they want on school nights. Your parents insist you be home before it gets dark. You know the other kids will tease you if they know you have a curfew. Using negotiation skills, can you and your parents work out a compromise?

_____

_____

_____

_____

_____

_____

_____

_____

_____

_____

_____

CHEROKEE FALLS JUNIOR HIGH SCHOOL

Educational Performance and Future Planning

Priority need: Learn how things studied in school will be useful outside of school

Goal: To help students manage time better

Management Objectives

1. By November 1st 8th-grade math students will learn skills for improving time management and share time management tips they have used successfully.

2. By November 2nd 8th graders will increase their awareness of how much time they spend in daily activities.

3. By November 7th 8th-grade students will have logged a week's accumulation of time management schedules to see where they can make improvements.

4. By November 10th any 8th graders who need additional help with time management can volunteer to work with a peer tutor on time management techniques once a week.

Outcome Objectives

1. After being presented with skills for improving time management, 80% of students will be able to share helpful time management pointers.

2. After participating in a class activity on balancing life, 80% of students will become aware of the time spent on daily tasks.

3. Upon keeping time management logs for a week, 70% of the students will be able to see where their time is being spent.

4. After working with peer tutors weekly on time management techniques, 80% of the students will demonstrate better use of time.

Strategies/Activities

1. Students will hear time management tips and share ideas about what has worked for them. The resource used is Korb-Khalsa, Azok, and Leutenberg (1992).

2. Students will complete the "Balance Your Life" handout to increase awareness of how much time they spend daily in leisure, individual care, unscheduled and free time, and school and work activities: Educational-1.

3. Students will keep a log for a week of how they spend their time: Educational-2.

4. Students who volunteer for extra help with time management will receive peer tutoring before school one hour per week.

Educational-1

Source: Korb-Khalsa, Azok, and Leutenberg (1992). "Balance Your Life" is a time management system that revolves around leisure, individual care, free and unscheduled time, and efforts in school and work activities. The chart is set up as a pie, with one-hour increments from 12 A.M. to 11 P.M. Activities are then written into the various time slots.

Educational-2

Name: Week of:

Time	Mon.	Tues.	Wed.	Thurs.	Fri.	Sat.	Sun.
6–7 A.M.							
7–8 A.M.							
8–9 A.M.							
9–10 A.M.							
10–11 A.M.							
11–Noon							
Noon–1 P.M.							
1–2 P.M.							
2–3 P.M.							
3–4 P.M.							
4–5 P.M.							
5–6 P.M.							
6–7 P.M.							
7–8 P.M.							
8–9 P.M.							
9–10 P.M.							
10–11 P.M.							

MILL CREEK JUNIOR HIGH SCHOOL

Lifestyle and Career Future

Priority need: Learn to make plans for developing abilities in career interest areas

Goal: To develop career awareness and explore careers of interest

Management Objectives

1. By February 1st students in 8th-grade English classes will be introduced to the importance of career awareness and career exploration in their lives after viewing a video on exploring careers.

2. By February 2nd 8th-grade students will take the Kuder interest survey to discover interest areas.

3. By February 3rd 8th-graders will begin researching two careers in their high-interest areas.

4. By February 4th English students will attend the school's career fair and hear people talk about their careers.

5. By February 5th 8th graders will be able to "job shadow" an employee in the field for half a day.

Outcome Objectives

1. After viewing the video on *Exploring Careers: What's Right for You?* (Sunburst Communications, 1997), 80% of the students will begin to understand the impact their future careers will have on their lives.

2. Upon completing and scoring the Kuder interest survey, 90% of the students will be familiar with interest areas and possible career choices.

3. After researching and writing about two careers, 80% of the students will be aware of requirements for future career possibilities.

4. Once students have attended the school's career fair, 80% of the students will have questions answered about careers in the local community.

5. By participating in the job shadowing project, 85% of the students will have a greater understanding of what takes place day-to-day in a career of their choice.

Strategies/Activities

1. All 8th-grade students will view the 33-minute video *Exploring Careers: What's Right for You?*

2. All 8th-grade students will take the *Kuder General Interest Survey* and will self-score their booklets.

3. All 8th-grade English students will research two careers in their high-interest category. A worksheet from *Dream Catchers: Developing Career and Educational Awareness in the Intermediate Grades* (1993), by Norene Lindsay, will be used: Lifestyle-1.

4. A career fair will be conducted at the junior high with 25 area professionals and technical employers invited to participate. Students will be given the opportunity to visit the booths of all exhibitors.

5. The 8th-grade students will job shadow someone in the community from first through third hours. Prematching will be done prior to the day of the actual event, with students bused to places of business in the community.

Lifestyle-1

Source: Lindsay (1993). Lindsay suggests the following questions in the form of a career data worksheet:

Job title: _____

What career cluster does this job belong in?_____

_____

Is the work mostly with people, things, and machinery or with data?_____

_____

_____

What are the working conditions? Describe the workplace.

_____

_____

_____

Would you likely be an employee or self-employed?_____

_____

_____

Describe the kind of work done on this job._____

_____

_____

_____

Describe the skills needed for this job._____

_____

_____

_____

_____

Where can the skills for this job be learned?_____

_____

_____

_____

_____

Can either a woman or man do this job? Explain your answer.

_____

_____

_____

_____

_____

DEER RUN ELEMENTARY SCHOOL

Goals, Objectives, and Activities

Personal, Behavioral, and Emotional Skills

Priority need: Develop self-awareness and self-acceptance

Goal: To understand the meaning of stress and how to deal with it

Management Objectives

1. By November 1st elementary students will be introduced to the topic of stress, hearing the book *Don't Pop Your Cork on Mondays The Children's Anti-Stress Book* by Adolph Moser (1988).

2. By November 2nd elementary students will brainstorm a list of stressors for them and other kids their ages, and participate in stress-relieving exercises.

3. By November 3rd elementary students will watch the video *Stressbusters* (Sunburst Communications, 1993b) to learn what they can do to deal with stress.

4. By November 10th elementary students who need additional help in dealing with stress can participate in small group counseling sessions.

Outcome Objectives

1. After hearing the book *Don't Pop Your Cork on Mondays,* 80% of the students will have a better understanding of stress.

2. After brainstorming ideas about what causes stress, 70% of the students will be able to identify stressors in their own and in their friends' lives, and will be able to participate in ways to relieve stress.

3. After viewing the video *Stressbusters,* 80% of the elementary students will understand ways they can deal with stress.

4. Of the students who participate in the small group counseling sessions for dealing with stress, 70% will report less stress in their lives.

Strategies/ Activities

1. Elementary students will hear the book, *Don't Pop Your Cork on Mondays.*

2. Students will be asked to volunteer ideas about what causes stress in their lives and in their friends' lives and will participate in stress-relieving exercises. A good resource of activities is *Building a Positive Self-Concept* by Marjorie Jacobs, Blossom Turk, and Elizabeth Horn (1988).

3. The 14-minute video *Stressbusters* will be shown to the class.

4. Small group counseling sessions on dealing with stress will be conducted weekly for four weeks. Parent permission will be secured. A resource with group sessions is *Skills for Living Group Counseling Activities for Young Adolescents* by Rosemarie S. Morganett (1990).

DEER RUN ELEMENTARY SCHOOL

Social Actions and Skills

Priority need: Learn to communicate with peers

Goal: How to deal with conflicts with others

Management Objectives

1. By October 1st elementary students will become aware of the term *conflict resolution* and the impact it has in their relationships with others.

2. By October 2nd elementary students will learn techniques for dealing with conflicts with others and will role-play situations.

3. By October 5th elementary students will have kept conflict logs for the week and will discuss various situations.

4. By October 6th students will play the game *Anger Control Bingo* (Martenz, 1997).

Outcome Objectives

1. After hearing what conflict resolution is and participating in an activity, 80% of the students will realize the benefits of resolving conflicts peacefully.

2. Once students have been presented with conflict resolution techniques, 70% will be able to role-play situations.

3. After keeping conflict logs for a week, 80% of the elementary students will be more aware of conflict occurring in their lives.

4. After playing the game *Anger Control Bingo,* 70% of the students will be reinforced in ways of controlling anger.

Strategies/Activities

1. Elementary students will be introduced to the meaning of conflict resolution and will participate in an activity. Students will be tied up loosely and must try to get untied; through this, they will learn that some problems are best approached through cooperation.

2. Elementary students will be presented with conflict resolution techniques and will role-play situations. A good resource is *Conflict Resolution for Kids* by Pamela S. Lane (1995).

3. Students will keep conflict logs for a week to see where conflict has occurred in their lives recently: Social-3.

4. Students will play *Anger Control Bingo*.

Social-3

Source: Lane (1995). Permission to photocopy is granted.

Conflict Log

Homework: This week, observe the conflicts happening around you and those in which you are involved.

What strategies did others (or you) use to resolve the problem?_____

_____

_____

_____

_____

_____

Write in your log a few lines (or draw a picture) about the conflicts you observed, then share one example with the group next session. _____

_____

_____

_____

_____

_____

_____

Take me with you to group meeting

DEER RUN ELEMENTARY SCHOOL

Educational Performance and Future Planning

Priority need: Learn more about counseling services

Goal: To acquaint students with the school counselor and his or her various roles

Management Objectives

1. By September 1st elementary students will become acquainted with the school counselor.

2. By September 2nd elementary students will learn about the various roles school counselors play.

3. By September 3rd students in elementary school will take a tour of the guidance office.

Outcome Objectives

1. After meeting the school counselor, 80% of the students will recognize who he/she is.

2. Once students have heard about the different roles of the school counselor, 80% will be able to take advantage of the services offered.

3. After students have toured the guidance office, 80% will know where to go for help in the future.

Strategies/Activities

1. The school counselor will read a handmade book about him- or herself to the students which includes pictures of him- or herself and his or her family.

2. The school counselor will share a brochure with students explaining his or her roles. This brochure will be taken

home to parents. The students also will receive a bookmark condensing the role information and giving the school counselor's name for future reference.

3. Students will take a tour of the guidance office and receive a piece of candy to promote positive feelings about the school counselor.

DEER RUN ELEMENTARY SCHOOL

Lifestyle and Career Future

Priority need: Learn about various jobs in the community

Goal: To generate interest in careers

Management Objectives

1. By March 1st elementary students will be introduced to the topic of careers as they listen to *Rappin' Up Careers* (Smith & Martenz, 1991) and learn some songs.

2. By March 2nd elementary students will complete activities in *Finding Your Tomorrow with Sunny* (Winter, 1996).

3. By March 3rd elementary students will participate in the *Alphabet Careers Game* (Sahlin, 1993).

4. By March 4th elementary students will hear professionals talk about their careers.

Outcome Objectives

1. After learning some rap songs about careers, 70% of the students will be aware of additional careers.

2. Once students have completed activities in the career booklet, 80% will have an idea of what they want to do when they grow up.

3. After participating in the *Alphabet Careers Game*, 80% of the students will be aware of additional careers by relating them to the alphabet.

4. After students hear professionals talk about their careers, 80% will have a greater understanding of what careers involve.

Strategies/Activities

1. Students will listen to a cassette of career rap songs and will learn some of the lyrics from *Rappin' up Careers*.

2. Elementary students will complete career activities—Career-2—in the booklet, *Finding Your Tomorrow with Sunny*.

3. Students will play the *Alphabet Careers Game*.

4. Various professionals will be invited to talk with elementary students about their careers.

Career-2

Source: *Finding Your Tomorrow with Sunny* by Casey Winter (1996). This booklet contains activities for elementary students that identify interests, future careers, and thoughts about future life pathways. The booklet is available from Kansas Association of Student Financial Aid Administrators.

Chapter 10

EXAMPLES FROM THE FIELD

Experience with several districts led directly to many of the specifics in this book. The following examples will show how each district and each experience is unique. Yet each district has found benefits at various stages of this process.

THE AMERICAN SCHOOL IN TOKYO, JAPAN

Kay Melton, Elementary Counselor

Contributions by Dr. John Bradley, High School Counselor
Tim Olson, High School Counselor
Steve Summerfield, Middle School Counselor

Editing, Dr. Ellis Melton, Curriculum Coordinator

Since 1902, The American School in Japan—a K–12 institute for the children of Americans and people of 35 other nationalities living in Tokyo—has taken pride in offering the very best in American education to its 1,400 students. In an effort to compare ourselves with the best stateside schools, eight years ago the ASIJ established a system for evaluating each of its programs. The cornerstone of this self-examination is a program audit, which occurs once in a six-year cycle. The outside auditor, who is selected by a committee of faculty and administrators, typically is a university professor with recent school teaching experience or a practicing teacher who is active in professional organizations.

In 1996, the counseling and guidance program was audited. After looking at several resumes, the faculty chose Dr. Don Rye as auditor, primarily because of his authorship of the first edition of this book. He visited the school for a week, looked at the program, interviewed stakeholders (students, teachers, parents, and administrators), and made specific recommendations for improvement.

Among other recommendations (such as moving the counseling offices and revising the classroom guidance program) he strongly advised ASIJ to establish a planning process. A central goal of this process was to build a base of common understanding related to the counseling and guidance program. In his report, Dr. Rye wrote, "Engaging all the persons and groups who benefit from counseling and guidance services in a decision-making and planning process will ensure that the efforts of counselors and others are focused on the identified and prioritized needs."

In addition to this program audit, the ASIJ accreditation agency, the Western Association of Schools and Colleges, sent a team of seven teachers and administrators to visit the school in the spring of 1995 as a culminating activity in the WASC reaccreditation process. While offering more general suggestions, the WASC committee also made specific recommendations regarding certain areas that needed improvement, which the school decided to incorporate into a master plan with Dr. Rye's audit recommendations.

The counseling staff (two high school counselors, two middle school counselors, and one elementary counselor) began the planning process by scheduling several meetings to define the mission of the program and determine which areas needed improvement. Although the elementary, middle, and high schools are on the same small campus, the five counselors had not been in the habit of meeting regularly, so these planning meetings had the immediate benefit of building a climate of collegiality.

In the fall of 1996, the counselors organized the first Counselor Advisory Committee. This committee included the counselors, one administrator, a parent, a classroom teacher, and two student representatives (a male and a female) from each division. One aim of the committee was to have more direct communication among the audiences served by the program—especially the parents. An overall goal of ASIJ for several years has been to establish better communication among all constituents. This committee helped us meet that goal.

As part of ASIJ's response to the Rye audit, two needs assessments were conducted during the 1996-1997 school year. The first was directed at students, the second was designed for parents. The results of the survey indicated clearly one common issue uppermost in the minds of students and parents: transition.

Because student turnover is about 30% annually, transition is a concern that affects every student. For new students, adjustment to a new school is the main focus of energy for the first few months of attendance. For students who learn they are leaving (which happens throughout the school year, but is concentrated toward the end of the year), saying goodbye and closing this part of their lives dominates the last few months of the school year. The rest of the student body is affected by the activities of both of these groups— sorting out making new relationships and losing old ones.

The other concerns expressed in elementary and middle school centered on friendships: how to make friends, handle peer pressure, communicate effectively with friends, and understand and belong to various social groups. In middle school, self-identity emerged as a chief concern, especially for bicultural students.

At the high school, the most often expressed concerns were about academic matters, career information, college selection, and preparation for college exams (SAT, ACT, and TOFEL). These issues are straightforward and easily addressed. Other expressed concerns were more complicated and personal; asking for help in these areas was less clear and more uncomfortable for the students. These issues included relationships with peers and teachers, feeling down and depressed, feelings of poor self-worth, stress, and pressure with friends and school.

The parent surveys in all divisions also showed transition as a big concern. Additionally, parent surveys showed concerns specific to grade levels:

- Elementary school parents wanted information about effective parenting, helping with homework, and helping children develop good study skills.

- Communication skills, setting boundaries, and cross-cultural issues were listed by middle school parents.

- High school parents wanted information about college selection, preparation for college exams (SATs), and stress management.

The survey made one thing absolutely clear: ASIJ serves an international community with a diverse variety of perceptions of the purpose of a counseling and guidance program. Although ASIJ is an American school with an American curriculum and a large percentage of American students, the student body comes from many cultures—including a large percentage of Japanese students.

The survey reminded us that the school counselors provide most of the formal emotional support to our families, because there are limited resources for expatriate families in Tokyo. Because of the rich data gathered in the student and parent needs assessments, the Counseling Advisory Committee is planning a needs survey for teachers and administrators.

About 14 months after Dr. Rye's audit, one of the two middle school counselors resigned. The counseling group strongly recommended to the administration that the replacement be a counselor with the sensitivity and expertise to work with needs and concerns of bicultural students and families from our host country. The proposal stated, "In carefully reviewing all of our student cases in the high school over the past three years, over 60% of the more serious cases have involved students who come from Japanese-speaking or bilingual (Japanese and another language) families." "Serious cases" included such issues as suicidal ideation and attempts, clinical depression, anorexia and bulimia, bipolar disorder, violence, substance abuse, and sexual promiscuity."

Having the Counseling Advisory Committee involved in processing the needs assessment information from students and parents gave the counseling staff specific information about bicultural/bilingual students and families and how much they need support from someone who understands their concerns.

The administration agreed, and changed the job description from a middle school position to one with school-wide responsibilities. About 20% of ASIJ families have at least one Japanese parent, and many of these parents do not speak English, although their children do. Even more than the language barrier, however, cultural differences often stand in the way of effective communication with counselors.

The school was fortunate to find a native Japanese counselor who was trained and has worked in the United States. She was hired to work in all four divisions: nursery kindergarten (which is located on a campus about 45 minutes away, and previously had no formal counseling support), elementary, middle, and high school. Her primary audience is students and families who have bilingual and bicultural concerns, although she will work with other students and families as well.

The Counseling Advisory Committee met four times during the first year. Participants were generally enthusiastic about the process. The students on the committee were equal participants, and that was positive both for them and for the adults.

As one of its first tasks, the committee developed this mission statement:

> The mission of the guidance and counseling program at the American School in Japan is to promote emotional health, interpersonal skills, physical development, and academic success in an international setting, where cultural sensitivity, transition issues, and family support are special concerns.

In the first year, all meetings were planned and facilitated by the counselors, which helped us accomplish the tasks of the mission statement and needs assessments. However, the counselors felt that members of the committee needed to assume more leadership in planning and facilitating meetings.

At the start of the second year of the planning process, the central problem was finding time to reorganize the advisory committee and continue with the plan. The counselors as a group are still grappling with the issues of prioritizing tasks and finding time. As with school counselors everywhere, they continually face situations that need immediate attention.

While convinced that careful planning on the front end will ultimately give them more time to see clients, blocking off two hours in the schedules of five busy counselors is a problem. The typical teacher, counselor, and administrator at ASIJ already works an 8- to 10-hour day on campus—aside from any preparation at home—plus occasional weekend coaching and in-service training. Breakfast meetings, after-school meetings, and sessions during staff development time have been explored. Most meetings of the counseling staff are off-campus to avoid the constant interruptions from telephones and knocks on the door.

Despite these difficulties, the process moves along. It is an ongoing process, of course; not one with a target ending date. We are already seeing the payoffs, however. Parents are more aware of what counselors do. The faculty sees the counseling staff as a team rather than as five harried individuals. The needs survey provided a reality check. After 18 months of what seems like very slow progress, the glacier is moving! The ASIJ counseling program is becoming a truly unified *program*, rather than the work, good as it has been, of five individuals.

BERRYVILLE PUBLIC SCHOOLS, BERRYVILLE, ARKANSAS

Linda Winkle, Elementary Counselor
Nancy Thompson, High School Counselor

It was fall of 1992 when we first became interested in developing a comprehensive K–12 counseling program. Our interest grew out of a need to stop rumors that had started over what elementary counselors were teaching. When a new counselor joined our staff and began using a Duso puppet, a small group of parents became fearful and alarmed that "New Age" philosophy was being presented through the program.

Since two of our counselors had recently completed a class with Dr. Rye at the University of Arkansas on developing a program, we decided to call him for assistance. He met with us on campus to help us get started. With controversy on the horizon, our superintendent was more than willing for us to begin.

Our next step was to purchase the previous edition of this book. We then began to put together a committee of concerned parents, staff, school board members, and community leaders. This was an easy process, since many people were already interested in the counseling program and concerned about the rumors. Once the committee had been selected, Dr. Rye met with them to explain what would be expected. We spent several hours together writing a rationale and philosophy, probably some of the most valuable results of our work. We then worked on our needs assessment, decided how to get a sampling, prepared mailings, and compiled results from our surveys.

After two years we had a complete set of written goals for K–12, as well as a philosophy and rationale. These have been very useful and were well worth the time and effort. Unfortunately, we have not carried the plan all the way to the end. This is due, in part, to several turnovers in the counseling staff as well as a change in superintendents. With these obstacles we soon found ourselves involved in busy day-to-day routines, added duties, and so on—a problem this process, when carried through, is designed to help us avoid.

Although we were not able to complete the process, we have benefited greatly from the steps we did complete: our philosophy, rationale, goals, and especially the input from community and parents. One of our main goals was to get our community involved and to gain their support for our program. As soon as they became part of the process, their fears were calmed. They began to understand and appreciate the role of a school counselor. We accomplished just that. We are thankful for all the help Dr. Rye and his book gave us.

LAKESIDE ELEMENTARY SCHOOL, USD #250, PITTSBURG, KANSAS

Mark Allai, Elementary Counselor

In the spring of 1990, I was given the opportunity to become the second of what would eventually be five elementary counselors in the USD 250, Pittsburg, Kansas, School District. I was asked to develop and implement a program at the largest elementary school in the district. The student population at Lakeside Elementary was 350 to 400 students in 17 traditional classrooms, K–5.

I was hired with no hours in counseling. In fact, I was under the impression that I was interviewing for a traditional third-grade position. The only stipulation in accepting the counseling position was that I would go back to school and earn my Master's Degree in elementary counseling at my own expense.

It was at this point that I was introduced to Dr. Rozanne Sparks at Pittsburg State University. Dr. Sparks quickly became an invaluable resource and guide in developing the comprehensive guidance program at Lakeside.

From the first day of school, I was not a classroom teacher. I was labeled a "counselor." Little did I know the changes that label would bring. I found I now had the time to listen to children, staff, and parents. I quickly realized that, in today's world, our children deal with many issues that require adult assistance. I found early that developing trust was the key to my success with students, teachers, parents, and administrators. I knew that to be successful I had to make regular student contact by conducting classroom lessons, small group sessions, and individual counseling and by maintaining high visibility before, during, and after school. I found that confidentially was a key to trust with the students, and I was lucky that most of the teachers understood this. I was very fortunate to have a principal who allowed me to be the "good guy," by not requiring me to carry out punishment.

Even though I had developed rapport with students, staff, and parents, most didn't understand exactly what my job was. I do not remember how many times I was asked, "Now, what exactly do you do?" Most of the staff and parents had not had an elementary counselor before; they had the image of a counselor as one who schedules classes, drinks coffee, teaches a class or two, eats lots of donuts, helps students decide on careers, and reads the newspaper throughout the day. I quickly found that educating staff and community was important if I was to be successful in providing a preventive counseling program for students.

While experiencing all these positives and negatives, I was learning in my graduate courses that I could build on the positives and clarify the negatives by implementing a comprehensive developmental counseling program in a K–5 setting. It was impossible in my district to implement a K–12 program for a variety of reasons.

The written material that came to be my guide in developing the successful comprehensive developmental guidance program at Lakeside was the previous edition of this book. With the help of Dr. Sparks and this book, I was able to establish a K–5 program in a sequential, effective manner.

Forming an advisory team was my first step. The support I had developed from teachers and the principal was very helpful in this step. The advisory team not only provided guidance, but also made the program "ours" instead of "mine."

The needs assessment process was difficult and time-consuming, but it was necessary in order to address the actual needs of the students, staff, and parents. Again, this assessment made the counseling program at Lakeside a *community program*, instead of *my program*.

With the guidance of the advisory team and the results of the needs assessment, I developed goals, objectives, and activities. Developing activities was time-consuming, and I gathered materials from peers in my graduate courses and from other elementary counselors.

Three years into the Lakeside program, we were addressing the identified needs through regular classroom guidance activities, small group work, and individual work with children. Through informational presentations at civic organizations, board meetings, and parent-teacher meetings, I communicated the importance of our planned program and of having a counselor in the school.

Having an activity guide that includes goals, objectives, and specific activities is invaluable whenever I meet with parents who have not participated in the planning process and who don't understand what a school counseling program does. Only twice have the activities in our program been questioned. Both times, I addressed this by asking the concerned parties to visit my office and view the materials. In addition, I invited them to visit a class to watch the classroom lessons. Having the planned program allowed me to communicate trust and openness to individuals having concerns.

Four years into the counseling program, advisory team members decided that learning how to deal with violence had become a need in our school. With the guidance of the team, I looked for a conflict resolution program we could implement. I called counselors in other districts until I found a program that was proven effective. In conjunction with a consistent school-wide discipline plan, I began teaching problem-solving skills in classroom sessions with the long-range goal of implementing peer mediators, kids helping kids solve their own problems.

In the next four years, violence in the school declined. In fact, we dramatically reduced teacher referrals to the office for discipline. Teachers had more time to teach. Kids got along. At Lakeside we found that by reducing conflict in the classroom, by teaching children about friends and how to communicate, and by giving them peaceful tools to work with, everyone could do the job they were hired to do. It became a much better place for everyone.

In the past eight years, I have become a certified counselor while maintaining my teaching skills. We have achieved success here because the elementary counseling program was planned, the community was involved, and the staff and students bought into the program. Any school can achieve success if they set reachable goals and objectives and have an effective resource to guide them.

Note: Mark and the team at Lakeside were so successful with their program that Mark has moved to a neighboring school, USD 249, in Frontenac, Kansas, where he will start a new program based on the specific needs of that district.

NEOSHO PUBLIC SCHOOLS, NEOSHO, MISSOURI

Tarrell Portman, former counselor
and current Ph.D. candidate

My experience with developmental guidance and counseling programs began during my counselor training prior to 1988. I had just graduated, with a master's of education degree in K–12 guidance and counseling from Southeast Missouri State University, when I accepted a position as 7–12 guidance counselor at a nearby rural school.

The realization of the enormity of the tasks facing me, slowly began to sink in. At a fall district counselors' meeting, a veteran school counselor said to me, "You don't know what lies ahead of you for the remainder of the year!" And she was right. Because of my lack of experience, I was not able to fully conceptualize my duties and responsibilities. They would go far beyond my idealism about being a school counselor.

By mid-September, I began to recognize the feeling of being overwhelmed. I was the only counselor in a building of 450 students in grades 7–12. I had the combined responsibility of being school counselor and coordinator of special education services for the building. My superintendent had instructed me that I had two primary responsibilities: (1) to get seniors scholarships and graduated and (2) to protect the principal. There was no written job description for a school counselor in the district.

I began to see the need for a plan. In the brief time I had been exposed to the Missouri Model Guidance Program in school, I had developed an interest. However, at that time, without practical experience, I was unable to see the application. Now I could clearly identify the need for developmental counseling programs.

I contacted the Missouri Department of Elementary and Secondary Education and ordered the *Missouri Comprehensive Guidance Kit.*

At that time, training sessions were scheduled in the spring semester. Our school signed up to attend. The superintendent, building-level principals, and counselors were all required to attend a two-day training. This required financial support from the school district and a commitment from the staff.

After training, I returned enthusiastic and implemented the model in grades 7–12, following the suggestions in the manual. Some aspects of the program were adjusted to fit the district and the results of the needs assessment conducted with students, parents, faculty, and staff.

Soon I felt secure in having a guidance and counseling developmental plan. I was able to serve 100% of the student population, have a programmatic approach to guidance, have accountability, devote my time fully to the guidance and counseling program, and identify student competencies related to counseling. I felt a sense of worthiness and fulfillment that I was serving students, teachers, parents, administrators, the board of education, and the community to the best of my ability.

Program management was now more clearly defined. I grew as a counselor and began to understand more fully what professionalism and counselor identity was all about. After two years, I accepted a position in a larger district. One of my questions during the interview was, "Is this district involved with the Missouri Comprehensive Model Guidance program?" I had embraced the program and wanted to remain in a district that integrated guidance and counseling programs into the overall curriculum. From that time on, when relocating I have asked the same question during interviews.

A few years later, I was asked to consider a position with the Neosho school district for the 1992-1993 school year. I had been a counselor for four years, and I had a strong commitment to the Missouri Comprehensive Model Guidance program. When I asked *the question*, I was told that the Neosho District did not use the model but instead used a developmental planning model developed at the University of Arkansas. At first, I was surprised, then I became curious. I accepted the interview and drove the 300 miles to Neosho.

On the day of the interview, I was met by Becky Brannock, a high school counselor pursuing a Ph.D. in counselor education at the University of Arkansas. As we toured the building we discussed the developmental counseling program in place at Neosho. We compared the two models and found they were quite similar. This was a fascinating experience. The faculty, staff, and administrators understood the importance of the counseling program. They even asked me specific questions about my philosophy of counseling, something I had not encountered before. The boundaries I had set were broadened. I accepted the position in May and moved to Neosho with my family.

Upon arrival in Neosho, I found that all three high school counselors were new to the district. Each of us had 3 to 4 years of counseling experiences and 12 to 13 years of experience in education. It appeared the district had searched for experienced counselors to continue their strong program. One of our first tasks was to explore the program already in place. An advisory council was in place, board policies had been written, and a needs assessment had been conducted. All components were available to the new counselors.

The importance for me of going into a school district that already had a developmental guidance and counseling program in place was that the program continued to serve the students regardless of changes in personnel. The developmental counseling program plan does not need to be placed on a shelf and forgotten until a three-year review, but can and should be an active, vital plan that benefits the populations served in the district.

As a minority student from a low-income family, growing up in a small rural community with one school counselor, I rarely sought help or even saw the school counselor, except from a distance. If my childhood school district had used a developmental program, my exposure to the counselor through classroom guidance or small group activities would have helped me. I might have understood better that someone was there to help me. I am fortunate that I learned this lesson later in life. My hope is that diverse children are learning it early from their school counselors.

SUMMARY

The examples in this chapter illustrate that the planning experience is always unique to the persons and community involved. The fact that each school will proceed in ways unique to the persons within it seems to support the planning model presented here. Having a model program for adoption by all schools based on a predetermined ratio of classroom guidance sessions or a percentage of time given to each major component oversimplifies the complexities of gaining support for locally valued program plans.

The planning process is the common ground that can yield a program that is comprehensive, developmental, and focused on the appropriate variables specific to each school. Furthermore, when a school-community collaborative effort is successfully concluded, stakeholders within the school and the community own the plan and are likely to commit resources to the plan.

A Beginning Point

When you are ready to begin planning, you should examine the current planning actions and resources in your school. The following list of questions can guide you and serve as a checklist of steps in the planning process.

1. What is the academic and professional experience of your counselors?

2. What K–12 planning mechanisms are presently used? Who participates?

3. Is the current planning process directly and explicitly congruent with or tied to other school planning efforts?

4. Is there an agreed-upon set of core beliefs about children, schooling, counseling, and guidance?

5. Is there a shared vision of what the counseling program will become?

6. Is there a written mission statement for the counseling program?

7. Is planning data-based? What data are used, and how?

8. Have goals and objectives been established, and are they related to identified needs?

9. Is the counseling program planned to be comprehensive and developmental from kindergarten through grade 12?

10. Do the evaluation methods employ accountability measures as well as process and outcome measures?

11. What is the nature and quality of contacts between counselors and teachers and between administrators and counselors?

12. What is the nature and quality of contacts between counselors and the community?

13. Does the district support the professional development interests and needs of its counselors through conference attendance, workshops, in-service training, and continuing education opportunities?

14. Are teachers involved in conducting classroom guidance groups, and are they encouraged to improve their skills in conducting these groups?

15. Are procedures in place for regularly reporting counselor activities to teachers, parents, and administrators?

16. Are the instruments and processes used for collecting evaluation data connected to the goals?

17. Are the performance appraisal procedures and standards designed to asses the counselor's contribution to the mission of the school?

18. Are the performance appraisal standards and procedures applied to counselors different from those applied to teachers and administrators?

BIBLIOGRAPHY

Begun, R. W. (Ed.). (1996). *Social skills lessons and activities for grades 7–12.* West Nyack, NY: Center for Applied Research in Education.

Brigman, G., & Earley, B. (1991). *Group counseling for school counselors: A practical guide.* Portland, ME: J. Weston Walch.

Brown, W. (1987). *Study power.* Iowa City: ACT Publications.

Capuzzi, D. (1988). Personal and social competency: Developing skills for the future. In G. W. Walz (Ed.), *Building strong school counseling programs* (pp. 49–90). Alexandria, VA: American Association for Counseling and Development.

Carr, J. V. (1996). Comprehensiveness of career planning: The third C—comprehensiveness. *Journal of Career Development, 23,* 33–42.

Chaskin, R. J., & Richman, H. A. (1993). Concerns about school-linked services: Institution-based versus community-based models. *Education and Urban Society, 25,* 201–211.

Christopher, J. C. (1996). Counseling's inescapable moral visions. *Journal of Counseling & Development, 75,* 17–25.

Colbert, R. D. (1996). The counselor's role in advancing school and family partnerships. *School Counselor, 44*, 100–104.

Cole, C. G. (1988). The school counselor: Image and impact, counselor role and function, 1960s to 1980s and beyond. In G. W. Walz (Ed.), *Building strong school counseling programs* (pp. 127–149). Alexandria, VA: American Association for Counseling and Development.

Collopy, D. C. (1993). A study of relationships among demographic factors, effective school characteristics, and school culture norms of educators in selected Iowa schools. *Dissertation Abstracts International, 54*(1–A). 38.

Council for Accreditation of Counseling and Related Educational Programs. (1988). *Accreditation procedures manual and applications.* Alexandria, VA: Author.

Dinkmeyer, D. (1989). *Parenting teenagers: Systematic training for effective parenting.* Circle Pines, MN: American Guidance Service.

Fairchild, T. N. (1994). Evaluation of counseling services: Accountability in a rural elementary school. *Elementary School Guidance and Counseling, 29,* 28–37.

Fairchild, T. N., & Seeley, T. J. (1995). Accountability strategies for school counselors: A baker's dozen. *School Counselor, 42,* 377–392.

Farr, J. (1994). *An introduction to job applications.* Indianapolis: JIST Works.

Gillies, R. M. (1993). Action research for school counselors. *School Counselor, 41,* 69–72.

Griggs, S. A. (1988). The counselor as a facilitator of learning. In G. W. Walz (Ed.), *Building strong school counseling programs* (pp. 41–48). Alexandria, VA: American Association for Counseling and Development.

Gysbers, N. C. (1988). Career guidance: A professional heritage and future challenge. In G. W. Walz (Ed.), *Building strong school counseling programs* (pp. 99–121). Alexandria, VA: American Association for Counseling and Development.

Haezebrouck, M., & Summerell, C. (1989). *School-based divorce groups.* Oakland, CA: Authors.

Hamilton, J., & Henley, T. (1988). *The Kansas guidance program evaluation guide resource packet.* Topeka: Kansas State Department of Education.

Hannaford , M. J., & Popkin, M. (1992). *Windows: Healing and helping through loss.* Atlanta, GA: Active Parenting, Inc.

Harrison, A. S. (1993). An evaluation model for middle school counseling and guidance. *Dissertation Abstracts International, 54,* 1677.

Hayes, R. L., Dagley, J. C., & Horne, A. M. (1996). Restructuring school counselor education: Work in progress. *Journal of Counseling & Development, 74,* 378–384.

Haynes, N. M., & Comer, J. P. (1996). Integrating schools, families, and communities through successful school reform: The school development program. *School Psychology Review, 25,* 501–506.

Hughey, K. F., Gysbers, N. C., & Starr, M. (1993). Evaluating comprehensive school guidance programs: Assessing the perceptions of students, parents, and teachers. *School Counselor, 41,* 31–35.

Jacobs, M., Turk, B., & Horn, E. (1988). *Building a positive self-concept: 113 activities for adolescents.* Portland, ME: J. Weston Walch.

Jensen, R. L. (1996). Comprehensive guidance: Implementation standards and career planning in Utah schools. The sixth C—coordination. *Journal of Career Development, 23,* 61–72.

Johnson, D. B., Malone, P. J., & Hightower, A. D. (1997). Barriers to primary prevention efforts in the schools: Are we the biggest obstacle to the transfer of knowledge? *Applied and Preventive Psychology, 6,* 81–90.

Keats, D. B. (1974). *Fundamentals of child counseling.* Boston: Houghton Mifflin.

Korb-Khalsa, K., Azok, S., & Leutenberg. E. (1992). *SEALS + Plus: Self-esteem and life skills.* Beachwood, OH: Wellness Reproductions.

Lane, P. S. (1995). *Conflict resolution for kids: A group facilitator's guide.* Muncie, IN: Accelerated Development.

Lee, J., & Pulvino, C. (1993). *Self-exploration inventories.* Minneapolis: Educational Media Corporation.

Lehman, G. (1996). A community's commitment to career planning for all: Clarity and commitment. *Journal of Career Development, 23,* 23–31.

Lindsay, N. (1993). *Dream catchers: Developing career and educational awareness in the intermediate grades.* Indianapolis: JIST Works.

Loesch, L. C. (1988). Is "school counseling research" an oxymoron? In G. W. Walz (Ed.), *Building strong school counseling programs* (pp. 169–188). Alexandria, VA: American Association for Counseling and Development.

Martenz, A. (1997). *Anger control bingo.* Warminster, PA: Marco Products.

Morganett, R. S. (1990). *Skills for living: Group counseling activities for young adolescents.* Champaign, IL: Research Press.

Moser, A. (1988). *Don't pop your cork on Mondays: The children's anti-stress book.* Warminster, PA: Marco Products.

Pritchard, M. (1994). *The power of choice: Communicating with parents* [video]. San Francisco: Elkind & Sweet.

Sahlin, J. (1993). *Alphabet careers game.* Warminster, PA: Marco Products.

Sandhu, D. S., & Portes, P. R. (1995). The proactive model of school counseling. *International Journal for the Advancement of Counseling, 18,* 11–20.

Smith, K., & Martenz, A. (1991). *Rappin' up careers.* Warminster, PA: Marco Products.

Snyder, B. A., & Daly, T. P. (1993). Restructuring guidance and counseling programs. *School Counselor, 41,* 36–43.

SRA. (1991). *KUDER general interest survey.* Monterey, CA: CTB/McGraw-Hill.

Sunburst Communications. (1993a). *Job interview skills.* Pleasantville, NY: Author.

Sunburst Communications. (1993b). *Stressbusters.* Pleasantville, NY: Author.

Sunburst Communications. (1997). *Exploring careers: What's right for you?* [video]. Pleasantville, NY: Author.

Swanson, D. (1995). *The resume solution: How to write (and use) a resume that gets results.* Indianapolis: JIST Works.

Tindall, J., & Salmon-White, S. (1990). *Peers helping peers.* Muncie, IN: Accelerated Development.

Walz, G. W. (Ed.). (1988). *Building strong school counseling programs.* Alexandria, VA: American Association for Counseling and Development.

Winter, C. (1996). *Finding your tomorrow with Sunny.* Emporia, KS: Kansas Association of Student Financial Aid Administrators.

Wolfelt, A. (1990). *A child's view of grief* [video]. St. Louis: Service Corporation International.

Index

ABOUT THE AUTHORS

Donald Rye, Ed.D., is Professor of Counselor Education at the University of Arkansas in Fayetteville. He received his B.S. degree in biology and education from Arkansas Tech University, and an M.S. and Ed.D. in Counselor Education from Indiana University. He has taught graduate courses in counseling at Tulane University, Murray State University, and in Bolivia, South America, Athens, Greece, and Saudi Arabia.

Dr. Rye has been an elementary and secondary teacher and a secondary counselor. He has received many service and recognition awards for his professional activities. He is a certified school counselor and a licensed professional counselor with specialization in clinical supervision. He has served seven years on the Arkansas Board of Examiners in Counseling and chaired the Arkansas Board for four years. He has consulted with schools in several states, Japan, and Malaysia on planning, implementing, and evaluating school counseling programs.

Dr. Rye lives near Elkins, Arkansas, on 20 acres, raises fish, has horses, and enjoys the Arkansas Ozarks with his wife, Shelia.

Rozanne Sparks, Ed.D., is Associate Professor in the Department of Psychology and Counseling and Director of Professional Laboratory Experiences in the School of Education at Pittsburg State University in Pittsburg, Kansas. She received her B.S. in Education from Southwest Missouri State University, and M.S. and Ed.S. degrees in counselor education from Pittsburg State University. She also received an Ed.D. in counselor education from the University of Arkansas at Fayetteville.

Dr. Sparks has taught music, mathematics, and computers in elementary and secondary schools in Missouri. She has been an elementary and secondary school counselor and an academic counselor at the university level.

She serves as a consultant for public schools and has presented workshops on planning and managing school counseling programs. She has received grants for conducting research in the public schools and has completed a series of research projects identifying characteristics of masterful teachers. Currently, she is involved in research identifying stages teachers experience, from the professional semester through the first three years of teaching.

Dr. Sparks belongs to counseling and education professional organizations at the local, state, and national levels, and has made presentations at all three levels.

DATE DUE

FEB 29 2002			
JUN 0 9 2006			

GAYLORD

PRINTED IN U.S.A.